P9-DFT-469

DISCOVERING
the PUBLIC
INTEREST

A HISTORY OF THE BOSTON BAR ASSOCIATION

DISCOVERING
the PUBLIC
INTEREST

DOUGLAS LAMAR JONES, ALAN ROGERS,
CYNTHIA FARR BROWN, JAMES J. CONNOLLY
AND DIANE KADZIS

CONTENTS

FRANK SITEMAN

THE LANDMARK MASSACHUSETTS
STATE HOUSE HAS STOOD ON
BEACON HILL SINCE 1796.

KELLER AND PEET ASSOCIATES

PREFACE

WHEN CONTEMPLATING THE HISTORY OF the bar in Boston, one immediately confronts nearly 300 years of professional growth and change. During that time, the legal profession in Boston, like the city and its people, changed dramatically. First organized in the 1760s, the Suffolk County Bar Association was the forebear of various incarnations of formal and informal bar organizations, including the Bar Association of the City of Boston in 1876, all of which form the lineage of the Boston Bar Association, which assumed its current name in 1946. This book seeks, in a short narrative, to tell for the first time the story of the organized bar in Boston and how that bar discovered for itself, its city and its society how best to act in the public interest.

In writing the history of the Boston Bar Association, we were lucky. The Bar Association generously opened its records to us, providing an unparalleled first-time look into the history of one of the oldest bar associations in America. We owe a special debt to the members of the History Committee of the Bar Association, chaired by Gene Dahmen, for enthusiastically supporting this project and sharing with us their initial research forays. We also want to thank Frank Moran, Executive Director of the Bar Association, and his staff for facilitating our work at every stage. As we concluded our research during the Association's renovations of 16 Beacon Street, Frank Moran and Carole Andrews skillfully arranged access to documents amidst a maze of construction workers.

But just as the history of the bar in Boston extends beyond what we think of as the organized bar, so, too, our research led us to other libraries in and around Boston. For their assistance in our research, we want to thank the staffs of the Social Law Library, the Massachusetts Historical Society, the Boston Public Library, Harvard Law School and the Thomas P. O'Neill Library of Boston College. We particularly want to thank the Massachusetts Historical Society for permitting us to quote from their collections. A special thanks is due to the Boston Athenaeum, the Bar Association's neighbor on Beacon Street, which generously donated rooms for us to use during the renovation at the Bar Association. Finally, this book was truly a collaborative effort by the authors, who shared ideas and materials and tested points of view with each other.

THE CHARLES RIVER FLOWS BY BOSTON'S DYNAMIC SKYLINE.

OPPOSITE: THE SUPREME JUDICIAL COURT BENCH AWAITS ITS NEXT SESSION.

Boston, Massachusetts
DLJ, AR, CFB, JJC, and DK

Origins and Visions

The Legal Profession in Early Boston, 1630–1800

THE SETTLEMENT OF the Massachusetts Bay Colony by the Puritans during the Great Migration of 1630 brought with it an enduring legacy of tension between the legal profession and the fabric of society. No strangers to the excesses of the power of the law under the Stuarts in England, the Puritans came from a tradition which sought to limit the discretionary power of judges, ecclesiastical courts and lawyers. Yet the Puritans of Massachusetts in the 1630s were deeply schooled in the ways of local law and custom, so much so that they chose for their leader John Winthrop, a lawyer with years of experience in manorial courts and in London. Winthrop, an eminently cautious and practical man, nevertheless viewed the settlement in New England as an errand into the wilderness that would by example convert England to the righteousness of the Puritan way. "We shall be as a City upon a Hill. The eyes of all people are upon Us," he told the passengers on the *Arbella*, presenting the idealistic, utopian vision of the Puritan experiment as they sailed for New England.

By the early eighteenth century, as Boston's population increased and the pace of commerce quickened, practicing lawyers flourished. As a distinct core of Suffolk County lawyers identified with each other, the Suffolk County Bar Association emerged in the 1760s as the antecedent of the Boston Bar Association. Though disrupted by Revolution, the eighteenth-century bar laid the groundwork for the organized bar in Boston.

COURTESY, NEW ENGLAND HISTORIC AND GENEALOGICAL SOCIETY

A RECONSTRUCTION OF BOSTON IN 1635 SHOWS THE ORIGINAL SHAWMUT PENINSULA AND THE SEVERAL HILLS AROUND WHICH EARLY SETTLERS BUILT.

OPPOSITE: MARY DYER, WHO IMMIGRATED TO BOSTON IN 1635, WAS EXECUTED IN 1660 FOR ESPOUSING THE "HERESY" OF QUAKERISM, BASED ON A LAW ACCORDING TO PURITAN BELIEFS.

THE LEGAL PROFESSION IN PURITAN MASSACHUSETTS

Lawyers played but a minor role for the first fifty years of the Massachusetts Bay Colony. The tension between the desire for an organized bar, the ideals of the Puritan experiment and the realities of the small, rural villages which comprised most of the Colony effectively minimized the role of the lawyer.

The original charter of the Massachusetts Bay Colony, granted by the English crown in 1629, gave broad powers to the General Court and the Court of

Assistants. Although neither body was primarily a court in the modern sense, the Court of Assistants assumed judicial functions. As early as 1635, some of the Deputies in the General Court voiced concern about the "want of positive laws" that allowed the Assistants, or Magistrates, to administer justice "according to their discretions." In response, the deputies sought to codify the Colony's laws in order to protect the fundamental rights and liberties of the people. Siding with the Magistrates, Governor John Winthrop argued that because they used God's word as the guide for their judicial decisions, the administration of justice was not arbitrary. The debate about what laws existed and how they should be administered was long and rancorous. Part of its resolution was the creation of inferior, or county courts, with jurisdiction over all civil and criminal cases not expressly reserved to the Court of Assistants.

COURTESY, COMMONWEALTH OF MASSACHUSETTS, MASSACHUSETTS ART COMMISSION

Governor John Winthrop presided over the Massachusetts colony for many years. Though an attorney by training, Winthrop in his role as Puritan statesman downplayed the place of the bar in adjudicating disputes, proclaiming rule by himself and the magistrates by "God's laws and our own."

The creation of a court system made it possible for men and women to litigate their differences, but it did not give rise to the emergence of a legal profession. Indeed, the shape and purpose of the law remained caught in the tension between the utopian community and the practicalities of everyday life. "The great questions that have troubled the country," Governor Winthrop told the deputies in 1645, "are about the authority of the magistrates and the liberty of the people." Because the Magistrates were elected by the people, Winthrop argued that a bond or covenant was established between the governed and the governors that was the basis for civil liberty. In the governor's formulation, only those who obeyed the laws enacted by the Magistrates had a right to civil liberties. "We shall govern you and judge your causes by the rules of God's laws and our own" and "your liberties [shall] be preserved, in upholding the honor and power of authority amongst you," Winthrop concluded.

Winthrop's authoritarian ideas were tempered by several general principles, including the idea that all governments were limited by the "fundamental law" and that traditional judicial procedures were a buffer against arbitrary power. Moreover, both Winthrop and the Deputies agreed that the laws of the colony should reflect "the conditions of the country and other circumstances." The General Court eliminated the English rule of primogeniture in favor of partible inheritance of real property and adopted a flexible rule for the allotment of property to widows. Writs were in English, not Latin, common-law forms of action were reduced to a few simple headings and Massachusetts had fewer capital crimes on its books than England.

At the same time, the courts adopted certain formal English forms of judicial process—the summons and the writs for attachment and distraint—and rules with regard to notice, costs, fees and appeals. Juries were impaneled from the out-set and the standard English terms for civil actions were used by the courts. Not all of the complicated distinctions made in English common-law pleadings were observed in Massachusetts courts during the seventeenth century, but more than a hundred different kinds of criminal offenses were codified eventually.

In 1641, the General Court met to "peruse all the laws, and to take notice what may be fit to be repealed, what to be certified, and what to stand." Working from a draft submitted by Nathaniel Ward, an Ipswich clergyman who had practiced law in London, the Deputies adopted *The Body of Liberties,* which was less a code of existing laws than it was a compilation of constitutional provisions, "the rites, freedoms, immunities, Authorities and privileges" that were to be safeguarded within Massachusetts Bay.

Seven years later the General Court completed a code of laws, *The Laws and Liberties of Massachusetts.* A compilation of public statutes and civil procedure, the code did not set forth every legal rule to be applied in the courts. Yet it was remarkable for what it did cover: crime, property, wages and prices, domestic relations and moral behavior. While a good part of English common law was incor-porated into the code, there were a number of new provisions that reflected the Colony's goals and ideals. The code provided the peo-ple of Massachusetts with "a Rule to walk by" for almost fifty years.

COURTESY, BOSTON PUBLIC LIBRARY, PRINT DEPARTMENT

SAMUEL SEWALL, FIRST CHIEF JUSTICE OF THE SUPREME COURT OF JUDICATURE (LATER THE SUPREME JUDICIAL COURT) FROM 1692 TO 1720, WAS MASSACHUSETTS' MOST PROMINENT JURIST. HE CONCERNED HIMSELF WITH THE QUALIFICATIONS OF LAWYERS AND JUDGES, FORESHADOWING FORMAL BAR ORGANIZATION.

Reflecting the strong bias against lawyers held by many English Puritans, the Magistrates prevented lawyers from practic-ing under the 1641 *The Body of Liberties.* But because judges were overwhelmed by demands for "advice and counsel in a legal way," the General Court eliminated this provision in the 1648 *Laws and Liberties.* Subsequently, it ordered in 1673 that "it shall be lawful for any…attorney…to sue in any of our Courts." Under this rule, a number of laymen practiced in Suffolk County courts, acting as "attorneys in fact," without special education or license. While many routine cases were han-dled smoothly by laymen, some of those practicing were rough and crude. For example, Benjamin Gibbs, who had an active practice in Suffolk County, once forcibly seized a suspected felon and "committed him…to the prison in Boston."

Another, Hudson Leverett, was fined "for his rash, indiscreet and dangerous speeches" in defense of his clients. In the hope of eliminating such raucous behavior, the General Court adopted an oath for attorneys in 1686. Lawyers were required to swear that "you will Do no falsehood," nor "plead no plea nor sue any suits unlawfully," nor "Demeane yourselves in the office of Attorneys." Six or eight lawyers took the oath that same year.

In 1701, the General Court required all attorneys to take an oath, to be "administered to them by the Clerk in open Court before the Justices of the same, at the time of their being admitted to such practice." The oath required lawyers to swear:

> YOU SHALL DO NO FALSEHOOD, NOR CONSENT TO ANY TO BE DONE IN THE COURT, AND IF YOU KNOW OF ANY TO BE DONE YOU SHALL GIVE KNOWLEDGE THEREOF TO THE JUSTICES OF THE COURT, OR SOME OF THEM, THAT IT MAY BE REFORMED. YOU SHALL NOT WITTINGLY AND WILLINGLY PROMOTE, SUE OR PROCURE TO BE SUED ANY FALSE OR UNLAWFUL SUIT, NOR GIVE AID OR CONSENT TO THE SAME. YOU SHALL DELAY NO MAN FOR LUCRE OR MALICE, BUT YOU SHALL USE YOURSELF IN THE OFFICE OF ATTORNEY WITHIN THE COURT ACCORDING TO THE BEST OF YOUR LEARNING AND DISCRETION, AND WITH ALL GOOD FIDELITY AS WELL TO THE COURTS AS TO YOUR CLIENTS. SO HELP YOU GOD.

COURTESY, HARVARD LAW SCHOOL ART COLLECTION

JEREMIAH GRIDLEY, "FATHER OF THE BOSTON BAR," ALSO ORGANIZED THE FIRST SUFFOLK BAR GROUP, SODALITAS, IN THE 1760S TO DISCUSS LAW AND PHILOSOPHY. MENTOR TO MANY DISTINGUISHED ATTORNEYS, INCLUDING JOHN ADAMS, GRIDLEY SOUGHT TO MAKE THE BAR AS PROFESSIONAL AS POSSIBLE.

The adoption of an oath for lawyers was one sign of the sweeping changes that had occurred in Massachusetts as a result of the Glorious Revolution of 1688-1689. Following that upheaval, Massachusetts gained a new charter, a royal governor and a Superior Court of Judicature. In 1692, five justices were appointed by the governor to the Province's highest court, including Samuel Sewall, who served until 1728.

The judges of the Superior Court took an oath that required them to "do equal law and execution of right to all people, poor and rich, after the laws and usage of this province." To achieve this end, the judges participated actively in cases before the Court. Sewall and his colleagues on the bench routinely swore in jurors and witnesses, heard and commented upon the evidence presented in court, instructed the jury and imposed punishment, if necessary. While the decisions of the Court were not recorded, Samuel Sewall noted that he and his brethren often articulated a rationale for their judgments, relying on biblical passages as well as legal precedents.

John Valentine and Thomas Newton, who were sworn in as attorneys by

Sewall shortly after they arrived in Massachusetts from England, were the leaders of the Suffolk bar in the late seventeenth century. Although Newton launched his career as attorney for the crown in the Salem witchcraft trials in 1692 by accepting the use of "spectoral" evidence, he later earned a reputation as a lawyer who carefully and skillfully applied English common law. As Attorney General, Valentine was responsible for trying the most serious criminal cases before the Superior Court of Judicature.

By the early eighteenth century, a growing number of college-educated lawyers appeared before the Court. Robert Auchmuty, a Scotsman trained at the Inns of Court in London, John Read, a Harvard graduate admitted to the bar in 1708 and Jeremiah Gridley, a Harvard graduate, legal scholar and mentor to a generation of eighteenth-century Boston lawyers, assumed the leadership of the Suffolk bar. Acknowledging the importance of such professional lawyers, Sewall told a grand jury convened in the new Boston courthouse in 1713: "Let them Remember they are to advise the Court, as well as plead for their clients." By the early eighteenth century, the nucleus of the bar in Boston was established.

THE LEGAL WORLD OF JOHN ADAMS

By the time of Sewall's death in 1730, the practice of law in Suffolk County was increasingly sophisticated, respectable and intellectually attractive. John Adams was typical of the young, bright, ambitious men who were drawn to the law in the mid-eighteenth century. In the decade after 1730, seventeen members of the graduating classes of Harvard and Yale chose to practice law in Massachusetts. Most of these young men were from families of "middling" means who had considered and rejected a career in the ministry. Embracing the ideal of civic virtue, they were committed to public service. Still, it was the steady growth of commerce that provided opportunities for lawyers. In order to buy manufactured goods produced by Great Britain, New Englanders increased the amount and diversity of their exports, expanded their commercial enterprises and invested in new shipyards and domestic industries. Under this economic stimulus, Boston grew quickly. Simple contracts and commercial relations constituted the bulk of a lawyer's work, with land cases a distant second.

COURTESY, BOSTON BAR ASSOCIATION

THE TOWN HOUSE (NOW CALLED THE OLD STATE HOUSE), WHICH WAS REBUILT IN THE EARLY EIGHTEENTH CENTURY. FOR MORE THAN 80 YEARS IT HOUSED NOT ONLY TOWN AND PROVINCIAL GOVERNMENT, BUT THE COURTS AS WELL. HERE SOME OF MASSACHUSETTS' LEADING JUDGES AND ATTORNEYS SAT AND PRACTICED FOR GENERATIONS.

"Let us look upon a lawyer," John Adams wrote in April 1756, to his friend Charles Cushing, who had asked his advice about choosing a profession. "We see him fumbling and raking amidst the rubbish of Writs, indightments, Pleas... [using] words that have neither harmony nor meaning. Besides," Adams added, "the noise and bustle of Courts and the labour of inquiring into and pleading dry and difficult Cases, have very few Charms in my Eye." Four months later, Adams rejected the ministry and entered into an agreement with James Putnam of Worcester "to study law under his inspection for two years." He vowed "never to commit any meanness or injustice in the Practice of Law," assuring himself that morality and religion were not contrary to the practice of law.

Adams's temperament and drive may have distinguished him from other law students, but the basic course of study he began in 1756 was the same throughout the colonies. Those two years saw him immersed in Sir Edward Coke's *Institutes of the Laws of England* and his *Commentaries on Littleton*, John Lilly's *A General Abridgement of the Law*, William Hawkins's *Pleas of the Crown (1716-1721)*, Thomas Wood's *An Institute of the Laws of England* (1720), as well as "Lesser Volumes" including statutes, reporters and practical manuals. He prepared his own pleadings book, copying the stilted technical language found in an English book of forms that he would later apply to the facts of particular cases. It was the characteristic feature of the common law that no claim could be redressed unless the facts could be made to fit one of the common-law forms of action. Adams also helped Putnam by making copies of the several forms of writs, promissory notes and other legal documents he needed. Finally, Adams attended court and talked well into the night with the lawyers who visited Putnam.

COURTESY, BOSTON BAR ASSOCIATION

SIR WILLIAM BLACKSTONE (1723-1780), BARRISTER AND LEGAL WRITER, WROTE *COMMENTARIES ON THE LAWS OF ENGLAND,* ONE OF THE SINGLE GREATEST INFLUENCES ON DEVELOPING AMERICAN LAW.

Because he believed that he lacked influential friends and social graces and that Putnam had not trained him adequately, Adams planned a three-part strategy to win approval from the Suffolk bar to practice law. First, he determined to read every legal treatise available so as to impress the senior members of the bar with his deep knowledge of the law. "Few of my contemporary Beginners," he noted upon his return to Braintree from Worcester in 1758, "have the Resolution to aim at much Knowledge in the Civil Law." Adams translated several pages from Justinian's *Institutes* each day and read Geoffrey Gilbert's *Reports in Cases in Equity*. Second, Adams rode to Boston to talk with young lawyers who had a "sense of the Dignity and Importance... of the Law" and to attend court. On one occasion, Adams shyly and anxiously sat at the lawyers' table in the Suffolk Inferior Court. Third, Adams learned from his neighbors. "I find," he noted with some surprise, "that as much knowledge in my

Profession is to be acquired by conversing with common People about the Division of Estates, Proceedings of Probate, Cases that they have heard as Jurors, Witnesses, Parties, as is to be acquired by Books."

His confidence somewhat bolstered by this last minute preparation, Adams went to see Jeremiah Gridley, the leading Boston lawyer, to ask what he needed to do to be permitted to practice law in Suffolk County. In response to Gridley's laconic "get sworn," Adams explained that he did not have a sponsor to recommend him to the court. At age twenty-three, Adams was thirty-three years younger than Gridley and in awe of him and the other senior members of the bar. But during the course of several hours of conversation, Gridley's kindly concern and sage advice put Adams at ease.

Gridley told Adams that he would speak to the bar on his behalf, explaining that the bar "must be consulted, because the Court always inquires if it be with Consent of the Bar" that an attorney be admitted to practice. Next, Gridley quizzed Adams, asking him what books he had read during the course of his law studies. Seemingly satisfied with Adams's intellectual preparation, Gridley offered Adams some advice: "pursue the Study of the Law rather than the Gain of it"; do not marry too young; and devote more time and energy to the law than to friends. Finally, Gridley urged Adams to visit with three other prominent members of the Suffolk bar—James Otis, Jr., Benjamin Pratt and Oxenbridge Thacher.

COURTESY, BOSTON BAR ASSOCIATION

Adams began his appointed rounds with Thacher. At the end of a long evening of discussion about "original sin and the Plan of the Universe," Thacher told Adams that Suffolk County already was "full" with lawyers. Undiscouraged, Adams next spoke with Pratt, who treated him roughly. Pratt wanted to know why Adams had not been sworn to practice in Worcester, where he had studied,

and why he did not have a letter of recommendation from Putnam. "No Body in this County knows anything about you," Pratt bluntly told Adams, "so no Body can say anything in your favour, but by hearsay." Although Pratt seemed satisfied with Adams's academic

As an active member of the Boston Bar, John Adams decried poor practitioners and observed with exasperation the inaction of many lawyers on the eve of the Revolution.

preparation, the young lawyer felt angry and worried. But in court that same day, Adams talked easily and comfortably with Otis.

On November 6, 1758, the day that the Suffolk Inferior Court was scheduled to adjourn, Adams and Samuel Quincy, another aspiring lawyer, waited in the court to be presented to the judges by the bar. Pratt again complained that no one knew Adams, but Gridley quieted Pratt by saying, "I have tried him, he is a very sensible Fellow." Later, Gridley told the Court that Adams had lived with James Putnam for more than two years, that he had "a good Character," that he had a good grasp of the "Principles of the Law," and, therefore, "the Client's interest may be safely intrusted in his Hands." The Clerk of the Court then administered the oath to Adams and Quincy. After being formally congratulated, the two young men invited the members of the bar to a nearby pub "to drink some Punch."

THE BUNCH OF GRAPES TAVERN, A FAVORITE OF THE SUFFOLK BAR IN THE 1760S AND 1770S, STOOD AT WHAT IS NOW THE CORNER OF STATE AND KILBY STREETS. IT WAS A HOTBED OF WHIG ACTIVITY, AND THOUGH HALF OR MORE OF THE MASSACHUSETTS BAR WERE LOYALISTS, SUFFOLK BAR FOUNDERS WERE WHIGS FAVORING INDEPENDENCE FROM GREAT BRITAIN, MAKING THE TAVERN A NATURAL MEETING PLACE.

A competing view of republicanism slowly took shape in the two or three decades after the Revolution. This new republicanism encouraged the individual acquisition of property and celebrated economic and political competition. While this ideology was not clearly articulated or widely accepted until after the United States Constitution was ratified, it had long been the central reality of urban life. John Adams recognized that Bostonians wanted the "conveniences and pleasures" that prosperity made possible and they would not be satisfied living in the "Christian Sparta" that his cousin, Samuel, envisioned. Because the law provided the technical means to release the creative energy of the people, lawyers were tied to the new republicanism.

COURTESY, BOSTONIAN SOCIETY

The conflicting ideological currents swirling around republicanism made the bar at once the object of hatred and the vehicle for economic opportunity. Because most lawyers believed that embracing the new republicanism was also the means by which they would achieve professional status, the conflict between old republicans and the bar was intensified.

Before the public debate over the shape of republicanism emerged, the Suffolk bar worked to revive its private professional status. In April 1780, seven members of the Association met at "Brother Hichborn's" to restore the Suffolk County Bar Association, which had been divided by the Revolution. The members issued an invitation to "all gentlemen of the bar who shall be in town" to attend meetings to be held at the new courthouse four times each year. The following year the meetings were moved to the Bunch of Grapes Tavern, which seems to have boosted attendance and produced greater conviviality. In October 1784, for example, twelve members attended what the secretary termed

JAMES OTIS, JR., WAS A SUCCESSFUL ATTORNEY WHO OPPOSED A NUMBER OF HIS PEERS, INCLUDING JOHN ADAMS, BY OBJECTING TO RULES FOR THE BAR. ADAMS BELIEVED HE WAS ALLIED TO "PETTIFOGGERS," OR UNTRAINED MEN WHO ADVERTISED THEMSELVES AS ATTORNEYS.

"a very social meeting." The year following, the Association invited the judges of the Supreme Judicial Court to a dinner, an event held in later years at James Vila's Concert Hall, a popular tavern at the corner of Hanover and Court Streets.

In the decades after the Revolution, the Association enacted rules to enforce a standard of educational achievement. The purpose of these rules was twofold:

to uphold the quality of the bar and to control the number of new lawyers admitted to practice. As it had in the past, the Association required that practicing attorneys who wished to take students into their office get the approval of the Association. No lawyer was permitted to take more than three students at a time, nor was he supposed to accept less than 100 pounds for a three-year course of study. Students who had read the law outside of Suffolk County were scrutinized by the Association to determine if their education conformed to Suffolk's standards. In July 1784, for example, the Association established an ad hoc committee to examine two applicants who had not graduated from college but wanted to study law with Christopher Gore. The committee—Robert Treat Paine, John Lowell and William Tudor—reported that the men "were well versed in the Latin and English classics," but had not studied "mathematics, ethics, logic and metaphysics." The Association rejected the two would-be lawyers.

Rather than dealing with these issues case by case, the Association adopted a clear set of rules at its meeting on January 28, 1800, that focused on the quality and quantity of education required of a lawyer in Suffolk County. Reflecting its local bias, the Association required an additional year of study for all potential law students who had attended a college other than Harvard. In addition, they insisted that a student must have studied for at least one year with a Suffolk County attorney in order to be recommended to the Court of Common Pleas. Lawyers from other states also were required to study for an additional year unless they had practiced before their state supreme court for at least four years. Finally, the Association created a standing committee to enforce its rules.

TORIES WHO FLED REVOLUTIONARY MASSACHUSETTS LEFT BEHIND PROPERTY AND REAL ESTATE THAT WAS CONFISCATED AND SOLD OR GIVEN TO PATRIOTS. ATTORNEY JAMES WARREN PURCHASED THE FORMER RESIDENCE OF GOVERNOR THOMAS HUTCHINSON IN MILTON THROUGH HIS CONTACTS WITH OTHER PATRIOTS.

The Suffolk bar also sought to regulate the activities of practicing attorneys and to help its members. In 1784, during an economic recession, a dozen members of the bar adopted a code of ethics that prohibited lawyers from soliciting business. About ten years later, the Association appointed a committee to investigate William Austin's charge of "dishonorable conduct" leveled at Luther Richardson, a bar member. With

COURTESY, BOSTON BAR ASSOCIATION

an eye on its members' pocketbooks, the Association made an unsuccessful stand against a law that permitted justices of the peace to try cases up to the value of four pounds, and in 1796, thirty-four lawyers agreed to adopt a new, higher fee schedule.

None of the private reforms implemented by the Suffolk bar after the Revolution protected it from the assaults made by old republicans. In 1785, for example, the Massachusetts legislature passed a series of laws designed to open up to all good republicans the practice of law. First, the new laws permitted the parties to a suit to plead their own cause or to use "the assistance of such counsel as they shall see fit to engage." Second, the legislation set minimum requirements for the admission of attorneys. Candidates were required to be of good moral character, support the constitution of the Commonwealth and be skilled enough to be useful in the practice of the law. The legislature's intent may have been to

open up the practice of law, but the bar subsequently convinced the courts that "counsel" should be interpreted only to mean a professional lawyer and that only formally trained lawyers should be admitted to the bar.

In the summer of 1786, Benjamin Austin, a leader of Boston's artisans and a political ally of Samuel Adams, published a series of articles in which he attacked lawyers and the existing legal code as contrary to the true principles of republicanism. "It has become necessary for the welfare and security of the Commonwealth,"

WILLIAM CUSHING, WHO TURNED FROM STUDYING FOR THE MINISTRY TO LAW, WAS ONE OF MANY DISTINGUISHED BOSTON ATTORNEYS INFLUENCED BY JEREMIAH GRIDLEY. HE SERVED AS JUSTICE OF THE U.S. SUPREME COURT (1789 – 1810), DECLINING AN APPOINTMENT AS CHIEF JUSTICE IN 1796.

COURTESY, BOSTON BAR ASSOCIATION

Austin wrote about lawyers, "that this order of men should be ANNIHILAT-ED." Austin and other old republicans feared that lawyers heightened the differences between the rich and poor, thus jeopardizing political equality and social harmony and making it impossible to achieve a virtuous republic. Austin proposed using ordinary citizens or referees to settle disputes, a practice reminiscent of the first decades of the Puritan settlement. After agreeing to be bound by the outcome, both parties would submit the relevant evidence to three prudent men. Because they had no interest in the quarrel, the referees would provide an honest and equitable solution, argued Austin. The legal code by which this system of justice would be guided would not rely upon the mysteries and ambiguity of the English common law. Austin insisted that the shape and purpose of the law be dictated by the genuine principles of republicanism and made easy to be understood by every individual in the community.

Several anonymous writers, including "Lawyer," "Democraticus," and "Zenas," stoutly defended the existing system. "Zenas" was widely known to be James Sullivan, a member of the Suffolk bar who had served in the Continental Congress and the Massachusetts General Court. Reviewing the history of the legal profession, Sullivan argued that lawyers were crucial to the maintenance of social order and the preservation of private rights. John Quincy Adams, a young law student in 1787, privately applauded Sullivan's counterattack. Although he personally felt the sting of Austin's assault on lawyers, Adams consoled himself with the thought that the future of the legal profession would "not be determined by the…artful misrepresentations of an insidious writer." Adams's assessment was correct. In the decade after the Revolution, the bar sometimes was criticized, but it continued to grow in strength and in stature. There were more than twice as many lawyers practicing in Suffolk County in the 1780s than there were on the eve of the Revolution. As Christopher Gore, a member of the Suffolk bar, put it: "Lawyers are growing into consequence."

DEMOCRACY AND ORDER

The Rise of the Informal Bar, 1800–1865

MASSACHUSETTS STRUGGLED throughout the 1780s to recover from the damaging effects to its economy brought about by the Revolution. Deflation forced prices down and reduced personal income. People who had bought goods or farmland or borrowed money when times were good found themselves in dire economic straits. The number of mortgage foreclosures and business failures rose sharply and litigation over debts large and small crowded the courts' calendars. Lawyers were busy, but not making much money, according to Harrison Gray Otis. By 1788, artisans, farmers and merchants alike believed that more commerce and innovative manufacturing was needed in order to achieve economic prosperity and political stability. For this reason, a majority of people in Massachusetts rallied behind the United States Constitution.

But the challenge of industrialization, economic development and democratization in the early nineteenth century led the bar to organize informally as it lost control over admissions standards. It continued to assert a leadership role in the state and the nation. After the Civil War, the bar reemerged in a more structured and organized form, laying the groundwork for the modern bar.

A NEW LEGAL AND CONSTITUTIONAL ORDER

Members of the Suffolk bar played a prominent part in the ratification of the Constitution. Nathaniel Gorham, one of two Massachusetts delegates to sign the draft of the Constitution in Philadelphia, boasted to James Madison in January 1788 that among the Federalists at the convention in Boston were "three judges of the supreme court [and] ten or twelve of the first characters of the bar." Among others, Christopher Gore, Francis Dana, Fisher Ames and Thomas Dawes, Jr., used rhetorical skills honed in the courtroom to help bring Massachusetts under the federal roof.

A handful of delegates opposed the Constitution, believing that lawyers were a threat to the new republic. Amos Singletary, a poor Berkshire County delegate tainted

The Hon.ᵇˡᵉ JOHN HANCOCK. Esqʳ

COURTESY, BOSTON BAR ASSOCIATION

LONG FAMED AS A SIGNER OF THE DECLARATION OF INDEPENDENCE, JOHN HANCOCK ALSO SERVED AS GOVERNOR OF MASSACHUSETTS AND AS A LEADER OF THE BAR. HE SIDED WITH THOSE WHO WANTED LAYMEN TO REPRESENT THEMSELVES, AND AGAINST FELLOW ATTORNEYS, BY SIGNING A LAW ALLOWING FOR SELF-REPRESENTATION IN 1790.

OPPOSITE: DANIEL WEBSTER WAS WIDELY ADMIRED AMONG MEMBERS OF THE BAR FOR HIS ORATORICAL POWERS. HIS INFLUENCE, AND LEGENDS CONCERNING HIS SPEAKING SKILLS, EXTENDED WELL PAST HIS OWN DAY.

COURTESY, BOSTON PUBLIC LIBRARY, PRINT DEPARTMENT

by the brush of Shays' Rebellion, spoke out angrily at the ratifying convention against lawyers and others he considered enemies of the people. "These lawyers, and men of learning and moneyed men," he charged, "gloss over matters so smoothly, to make us, poor illiterate people, swallow down the pill" of a more powerful national government. Working men in Boston, however, cheered when the good ship *Federal Constitution* was hauled through the streets on February 8, 1788, following the ratification of the Constitution by Massachusetts.

Because the postwar recession lasted well into the 1790s, complaints continued to be made about the inefficiency and expense of trials and the fees charged by lawyers. John Gardiner, a Boston-born lawyer trained in England, who returned after the Revolution to manage a huge tract of land in Maine, launched an attack on the legal system and the Suffolk bar in 1790. A member of the House of Representatives, Gardiner called for more than fifty changes in Massachusetts law and legal practice, including the abolition of the common law and of bar associations. While he may have spoken for many of the poor, frustrated squatters he represented, Gardiner also nursed a personal grudge. In 1784, the Suffolk bar refused to permit his son to study law, judging him deficient in "mathematics, ethics, logic, metaphysics," and, though unspoken, patriotism.

Gardiner's intemperate speeches alienated all but a few legislators. By a narrow margin, the House agreed to keep open the practice of law to laymen and to permit people to defend or prosecute their own causes. Thomas Dawes, Jr., urged Attorney General Robert Treat Paine to advise Governor John Hancock to veto the bill. "The Courts will be worse than Town Meetings," Dawes grumbled. Despite this opposition from the Boston bar, Hancock signed the measure into law in the spring of 1790, noting that it was a traditional republican right to represent oneself in court.

When Theodore Sedgwick, a conservative Stockbridge attorney, was appointed to the Supreme Judicial Court in 1803, he advocated reform of the judicial system, arguing that people would "avoid being entangled" by a complex and awkward judicial system. Only if the system were "wise, simple, and expeditious" would people consider it "the most certain means of obtaining justice." The legislature quickly acted upon Sedgwick's recommendations. In 1803 the General Court enlarged the jurisdiction of the Court of Common Pleas and allowed it to regulate appeals. The following year the legislature permitted a single Supreme Court judge on circuit to preside over all jury trials except those involving capital crimes or divorce, and to dismiss those appeals considered "frivolous, immaterial, or intended for delay." Two years later, the legislature took a step to end what Sedgwick termed the "mischievous uncertainty" about what the

COURTESY, BOSTON PUBLIC LIBRARY, PRINT DEPARTMENT

RUFUS CHOATE WAS PERHAPS THE GREATEST ATTORNEY IN THE CLASSICAL TRADITION DURING THE FIRST HALF OF THE NINETEENTH CENTURY. HE BELIEVED THAT THE PURPOSE OF THE LAW WAS TO PRESERVE THE STATE AND THE SOCIAL ORDER, NOT TO CHANGE THEM.

law was, by providing for the publication of the Supreme Judicial Court's decisions.

THE SUFFOLK COUNTY BAR ASSOCIATION IN THE EARLY NINETEENTH CENTURY

Boston's leading attorneys met in April 1804 to reorganize themselves, charging a committee consisting of Edward Grey, John Phillips, William Sullivan, Charles Paine and Thomas O. Selfridge to formulate regulations for admission to the Suffolk County bar. Meeting next in March 1805, the Suffolk County bar approved rules governing bar admission, fees, practice and law student regulations. The exclusive nature of the organization was apparent: bar membership was open to only those admitted to practice before the Supreme Judicial Court, a separate process involving previous admission to and years of practice before the Court of Common Pleas. Moreover, two grades of lawyers, attorneys and counsellors, were distinguished in discussing admission to the Supreme Judicial Court; to become a counsellor required practice as an attorney before the Court for a number of years. Those accepted before the Supreme Judicial Court were probably a very small group, perhaps no more than fifty or sixty.

Most business was delegated to a standing committee of five to be elected by the whole body. The standing committee in turn had sole responsibility for electing the bar's president, though the whole bar elected the secretary-treasurer. The power to admit applicants to the bar, at all levels, and to vote on various other issues of interest to the bar was almost entirely turned over to this small group. Its power was magnified after 1811, when the Supreme Judicial Court gave permission for student approval to reside entirely with the committee. In some years, the annual bar meeting was omitted because of the absence of key people or for other reasons not enumerated, leaving the impression that real business remained with the standing committee. Finally, it is clear the individuals chosen for this committee were the powers behind the Boston legal establishment, at least by the 1820s; in 1822, the quorum for standing committee meetings was set at one, a figure apparently never questioned.

Requirements for practice after 1808 included a college degree and three years of approved study with a Supreme

COURTESY, BOSTON BAR ASSOCIATION

AN 1801 VIEW OF STATE STREET, A BUSY COMMERCIAL CENTER, SHOWS THE OLD STATE HOUSE AFTER IT HAD CEASED TO BE THE CENTER OF GOVERNMENT. JUST BEHIND THE OLD STATE HOUSE IS COURT STREET, ONE OF THE NEW CENTERS OF LEGAL ACTIVITY.

Judicial Court practitioner, or seven years of "literary pursuits" (apparently to fill in for high school and college) and the three years of office study. Students paid $150 a year for this privilege (raised to $500 in 1810). This sum alone indicates the social status most young men would have to have had to pursue the law, and may be one of the reasons bar admission requirements were loosened in the 1830s. While the rules stated that only three students per practitioner could have their years of study count toward the total, a number of bar members routinely had more than three students approved to study with them, without reference to this limit, indicating either that certain attorneys were exempt from this rule or that enforcing it proved unworkable or unpopular.

The five-man standing committee included senior, well-respected bar members. The first group—Christopher Gore, Joseph Hall, Daniel Davis, Charles Jackson and Rufus G. Amory, included several notable attorneys. Davis, for example, was Solicitor General of the Commonwealth, while Gore was probably the longest-practicing lawyer then in Suffolk County. From their number they chose Gore as president, a position he filled until 1810, when Davis, who was often called the bar's "senior member," took his place from 1810

A LEGISLATIVE DEBATE DURING THE EARLY NINETEENTH CENTURY OFTEN DREW PUBLIC INTEREST. IN MASSACHUSETTS THE STATE LEGISLATURE INCREASINGLY TOOK A ROLE IN REGULATING THE BAR.

until 1814. It may be that the most senior or most respected bar member was *ipso facto* elected, as in the case of Lemuel Shaw, who served as president from 1827 to 1830.

The members of the Suffolk bar sought to extend their reach to create a statewide set of bar regulations, as recorded in the vote of the first 1805 meeting to distribute the rules to all counties. The response of other bar associations is not recorded; it is likely that they ignored it as they had done in the past. Yet the dream of a unified bar would be pursued much later by Boston bar members.

Despite the scope of the rules, problems in regulating the bar remained. A dispute about recovery of costs brought before the standing committee in 1810 found that group reluctant to adjudicate. Instead, they decided that there was "no sufficient usage or unified custom" that would enable them to decide the issue. The bar responded more vigorously, however, to questions of the irregular preparation of law students, and declined to admit several men to the bar whose preparation or prior work as attorneys in other jurisdictions made them suspect.

The Suffolk bar interacted socially in three broad areas: the annual dinner and address, which at times were well attended and at times canceled or of limited interest; recognition of and attendance at the funerals of certain judges and distinguished members of the bar; and the disbursement of funds to assist bar members and their families who were in financial distress. The guild-like nature of the Suffolk bar was clearly shown as families as well as attorneys could appeal to the legal brethren for relief.

The bar considered a report in 1814 regarding the problems posed by having a Circuit Court of Common Pleas for Suffolk County. The report blamed the circuit system for holding up, even denying, justice, and recommended a permanent court in Suffolk County be established, noting the success of the Municipal Court in expediting justice for the Town of Boston. Though no formal record of the acceptance of this idea is in the bar's own records, a Court of Common Pleas was soon organized for Suffolk County, and it is probable that the Bar Association had a considerable role in that decision. The other issues which the bar took up were largely those of improvements to bar seating or the courtrooms, with uneven success.

THE COMMON LAW TRADITION
V. THE CODIFICATION MOVEMENT

In the eighteenth century, the common law was conceived of as a body of fixed doctrine to be applied in order to achieve a fair result between litigants in

COURTESY, BOSTON BAR ASSOCIATION

private cases. In contrast, judges in the nineteenth century placed a central role in directing the course of social change. Judges used common law adjudication as a process for making and not merely discovering legal rules, a process that accepted the emerging social and economic realities. Increasingly, arguments attuned to the new economic realities undercut the old common law's dependency on form, in favor of content. By 1820, the legal landscape bore little resemblance to what had existed when the republic was created forty years earlier. Lawyers and judges increasingly used the law as a tool to accommodate change and to promote what they determined to be the good of the Commonwealth. The people of the Commonwealth expected their government to participate actively in their economic affairs, Lemuel Shaw told the Suffolk bar in 1827. The notion that the economy should be permitted to assume its own shape or that individuals should be completely free to pursue their selfish interests was "manifestly erroneous." As used by Shaw, the commonwealth idea encouraged the state to govern the economy in the public's best interest.

J OHNSON HALL WAS DESIGNED BY CHARLES BULFINCH AND BUILT IN 1810 TO HOUSE THE SUPERIOR COURT. DESPITE THE COURT'S GROWTH MOST PERSONNEL WERE STILL THERE IN 1848. ONCE THE COURT MOVED INTO LARGER QUARTERS, THE BUILDING BECAME OLD CITY HALL.

COURTESY, BOSTON BAR ASSOCIATION

In contrast to Shaw, reformers wanted to reduce judge-made law by substituting written legal codes for the common law, thereby codifying legal rules for everyone. They insisted that the task of creating and adapting the law belonged to elected legislators, not judges. Lawyers were divided by the codification issue. Writing in the *North American Review* in 1827, William H. Gardiner, a member of the Suffolk bar, lamented that the division between lawyers over codification had initiated a "fierce and interminable war."

Robert Rantoul, Jr., led the challenge against judge-made common law in Massachusetts. Born in Beverly, Rantoul graduated from Harvard College in 1826, read the law with John Pickering in Salem and was admitted to the Essex County bar in 1829. Following a successful career as a state representative, Rantoul moved to Boston in 1840 to practice law and to pursue legal reform, including the movement to codify the law.

In Scituate on the Fourth of July in 1836, Rantoul spelled out his criticisms of the common law and called for codification. "The Common Law sprang from the Dark Ages," began Rantoul. It had its origin in "folly, barbarism, and feudality" and was used by an armed elite to control the powerless, ignorant people. "In our own age," argued Rantoul, "judges use the common law to override legislative power, the enlightened voice of the majority of the people." The common law, he continued, "is subversive of the fundamental principles of free government." Judges who made law not only usurped legislative power, but ran "riot beyond the confines of legislative power." Judge-made law is really special legislation; each ruling is made according to the "bias which the coloring of the particular case gives," not according to the needs of an entire class of people. Rantoul concluded that the only way to reform the legal system was to codify the whole body of law.

The vast majority of the Suffolk bar were appalled by Rantoul's campaign against the common law. The bar cherished the traditional common law system, believing that it was more than a body of principles, more than ancient usage bound to English history. The common law was a profound and universal exploration of moral and philosophical truth, the basis of which was Christianity. The moral quality of the law not only gave the profession its transcendent dignity, but assured a citizen's fundamental right to life, liberty and property. The principles underlying the common law were perfect and comprehensive and made possible exact and equal justice.

As a solution to the codification controversy, Justice Joseph Story, also the Dane Professor of Law at Harvard Law School, proposed to the Suffolk bar that it initiate "a gradual digest, under legislative authority," of the settled portions of the common law. Specifically, he advocated revising the existing statute law and codifying that part of the common law that the courts had reduced to agreed-upon principles. Judges were best suited for this task, possessing the experience, knowledge and time to undertake the complex task of deriving principles from the long history of intricate human actions. But, if the best efforts of lawyers and judges failed to produce a single, agreed upon principle, the legislature should "fix a rule."

In January 1836, Governor Edward Everett appointed Story to head a state commission on codification. Story accepted the appointment, believing that the "present state of popular opinion here makes it necessary to do something on that subject." The editors of the *American Jurist and Law Magazine* agreed. "A few years ago," the writer commented, "codification had a direful import to the conservative party in jurisprudence ... since some of its early champions were sturdy radicals in legal reform. In this view codification was another name for

COURTESY, BOSTON PUBLIC LIBRARY, PRINT DEPARTMENT

Grand Centennial March.

As performed by the

BOSTON BANDS.

Composed & respectfully dedicated to the

HON. HARRISON GRAY OTIS,

Mayor of Boston

BY

CH: ZEUNER.

Boston

Published by C. Bradlee 164 Washington Street.
1830.

A BUCOLIC IMAGE OF THE STATEHOUSE AND BOSTON COMMON CHARACTERIZED THE SMALL-TOWN NATURE OF BOSTON AS LATE AS THE 1840S. THE MODERNIZING TRENDS THAT PERMANENTLY CHANGED AMERICAN SOCIETY, HOWEVER, WERE ALREADY BEING FELT IN THE LEGAL PROFESSION.

Juridical revolution." But now, with revision in the hands of a moderate like Story, the writer concluded, the alarm has subsided.

Story opened his 1836 report to Governor Everett with an eight-page summary of the common law and a modest plan for its reform and codification. Pointedly omitting property rights, Story recommended codification in three areas—the common law of crimes, civil procedure and evidence, and several areas of commercial law. The rules and doctrines of the common law in these areas are "spread over many ponderous volumes" and "authorities are to be found on each side of a point." Four or five lines of text in a code, "stating the true general rule," would clarify the law for everyone and reduce the workload of lawyers and judges. Finally, Story recommended appointing five commissioners "of high standing in the profession" to carry out the job.

COURTESY, BOSTON PUBLIC LIBRARY, PRINT DEPARTMENT

A commission was appointed by the legislature to codify the criminal law, but the legislature rejected the commission's proposal

MODERNIZATION IN THE EARLY TO MID-NINETEENTH CENTURY LED TO A HOST OF NEW LEGAL ISSUES AND PROBLEMS. IN THIS COLLECTION OF BANK NOTE ILLUSTRATIONS, THE SYMBOLS OF CHANGE ARE MANY: RAILROADS, TRADING SHIPS, AND SEAPORT COMMERCE ARE AMONG THE SCENES. THE QUESTIONS RAISED BY MODERNIZATION OFTEN LANDED IN THE COURTS, A PRACTICE THAT CONTINUES TODAY.

in 1844. Among other arguments, legislators contended that there was less need for codification because Story's treatises on the law and the published opinions of the Supreme Judicial Court had already created written access to the common law.

In 1849, a second legislative commission recommended a simplified code of civil procedure. Adopted three years later, the Practice Act was a far cry from the streamlined Code of Civil Procedure written by David Dudley Field and enacted by New York

IN THE
INTEREST OF THE
PROFESSION

Organizing the Boston Bar, 1865–1900

A STORIED PAST SHAPED the Boston bar's approach to the future in the closing decades of the nineteenth century, a past that proved inescapable as the city's leading lawyers attempted to formulate a response to changes in society and in their profession. They reorganized to pursue their goals more effectively, but by aiming to restore the past rather than dealing with the present and future. In their minds, the new Bar Association of the City of Boston constituted a formal expression of the authority long considered to rest with the community's leading lawyers. The mantle of leadership, however, no longer remained so securely balanced on the shoulders of a few. Faced with a society and a profession in the midst of profound change and hampered by their nostalgic vision, the founders of the Association made little headway in their efforts to maintain the dignity of their profession and reform the legal system. Frustrated, younger members sought to remake the Association on more egalitarian grounds only to be thwarted by its more conservative elements. Thus, even as the Association stood on the threshold of a new century, the ideas of the old one refused to give way.

THE BAR IN BOSTON AFTER THE CIVIL WAR

The problems that plagued the Bar Association in the late nineteenth century had their roots in the period before its founding. The leaders of the Boston bar after the Civil War believed that the bar should have a natural leadership, that those leaders should occupy a position of public prominence, and that the entire legal profession should receive the respect and deference of the whole community. As each of these myths began to crumble, Boston's legal profession and its leaders viewed the future with growing unease.

Every aspect of life in the United States was transformed in the decades after the Civil War. Between 1865 and 1900, Massachusetts became an urban state, with 86

COURTESY, BOSTON BAR ASSOCIATION

THE HISTORY OF A CONTINUOUS BOSTON BAR ASSOCIATION BEGINS IN 1876, WHEN AT LEAST 37 EMINENT ATTORNEYS MET IN THE SUPERIOR COURT ROOM TO LAUNCH THE BAR ASSOCIATION OF THE CITY OF BOSTON.

OPPOSITE: THESE MATERIALS FROM LEMUEL SHAW'S MANUSCRIPTS AND FROM THE COLLECTIONS OF THE SOCIAL LAW LIBRARY OF BOSTON RECALL AN AGE BEFORE MODERN TECHNOLOGY: HANDWRITTEN PLEADINGS, FORM BOOKS, AND THE INFLUENCE INDIVIDUALS SUCH AS SHAW COULD HAVE ON THE LEGAL PHILOSOPHY AND PRACTICE OF AN ENTIRE STATE.

KELLER AND PEET ASSOCIATES, SOCIAL LAW LIBRARY, BOSTON

percent of its population in 1900 living in cities. The population of Boston jumped from 178,000 in 1860 to 560,000 in 1900, nearly one-half of whom were foreign-born. For the most part, immigrants to Massachusetts swelled the ranks of the working classes who sought jobs in factory towns and cities. Boston, the region's financial hub, was ringed by factory towns such as Fall River, Lawrence, Lowell and Lynn, all of which were connected by a growing network of railroads.

If looking ahead unnerved the leading lawyers of Boston, looking back upon their predecessors filled them with great pride. They saw men who not only led their profession, but led their community and their nation as well. Lawyers like Daniel Webster and Rufus Choate, judges like Joseph Story and Lemuel Shaw not only succeeded within the legal realm but occupied exalted positions in the larger social and political setting as well. From John Adams on, few cities in the republic had produced more important lawyers and jurists than Boston. Such was the legacy that greeted those who occupied the higher ranks of the city's bar in

X — COURT AND TREMONT STREETS FROM SCOLLAY SQUARE.
REPRODUCED FROM A CUT IN THE PUBLIC LIBRARY OF THE CITY OF BOSTON.
Issued with Bulletin, October, 1894.

COURTESY, BOSTON PUBLIC LIBRARY, PRINT DEPARTMENT

A VIEW FROM SCOLLAY SQUARE OF COURT AND TREMONT STREETS SHOWS THIS AREA AS IT APPEARED IN THE MID-NINETEENTH CENTURY. LEGAL AND COMMERCIAL CONCERNS WERE STILL CONCENTRATED IN THIS NEIGH-BORHOOD OF BOSTON, AS THEY HAD BEEN SINCE COLONIAL TIMES.

the 1860s.

The men who led Boston's bar in the 1860s and 1870s came of age professionally in the era of Choate and Shaw. Foremost among them was Sidney Bartlett, who studied law with Nathaniel Morton Davis and in 1820 entered the law office of Lemuel Shaw. The two men formed a partnership in 1820 that lasted until Shaw's elevation to the Supreme Judicial Court in 1830. Bartlett gradually rose to a position of leadership in his profession which he held until his death in 1889, earning by his longevity the title "the Nestor of the Bar." A number of others accompanied Bartlett in his climb, notably his cousin William G. Russell, Charles Greeley Loring, Benjamin R. Curtis, George Stillman Hillard, and Ebenezer Rockwood Hoar, all of whom received their legal training early in the century. Together they came to constitute the highest tier of Boston's legal profession.

Just as Bartlett and others were situated in the upper echelons of the legal community, some lawyers found themselves on the middle rungs of the legal ladder. These middling lawyers handled private disputes, divorces, contracts, and managed the affairs of business and coordination. Lawyers who occupied the second tier of Boston's legal hierarchy had widely different backgrounds and careers. Marquis Dickinson, for example, graduated from Amherst College in 1862, read the law with a local attorney and finished his education at Harvard Law School. Admitted to the Suffolk bar in 1867, he became a partner in the firm Hillard, Hyde and Dickinson and, by litigating a large number of important cases for the West End Railway Company, amassed a considerable fortune. Other lawyers like Alfred D. Chandler practiced corporate and patent law.

COURTESY, BOSTON BAR ASSOCIATION

AS A YOUNG BOSTON ATTORNEY, OLIVER WENDELL HOLMES WAS ACTIVE IN EFFORTS TO UPGRADE THE BAR, AND JOINED THE CALL IN 1866 FOR A BAR ORGANIZATION. HIS DISTINGUISHED CAREER LED TO AN APPOINTMENT TO THE U.S. SUPREME COURT.

At the bottom of the legal ladder were those lawyers—perhaps one-half of the Suffolk bar—who handled the thousands of cases each year heard in the municipal and police courts. Edwin Wright and Seth Webb, for example, graduated from college in the 1840s, prepared for the bar by reading the law with a Suffolk attorney and then launched their own general practices. Eventually appointed a judge of the Boston Police Court, Webb formed several short-lived partnerships, but for nearly his entire career he had his own office in Brighton. Later in the century, Irish lawyers, Thomas Gargan and John R. Murphy followed well-worn career paths to respectability and moderate financial success. Gargan was just nineteen years old when he was commissioned a second lieutenant in the 55th Massachusetts Regiment in 1863. Following his return from the War, he won election to the Massachusetts House of Representatives, served as a delegate to the Democratic National Convention and presided over the Boston Charitable Irish Society. In 1873, Gargan graduated from Boston University Law School, read law with Henry W. Paine (a founder of the Boston Bar Association) and was admitted to the Suffolk bar in 1875. Murphy was born in Boston in 1853, attended Boston College and graduated from Georgetown University in 1872. He taught Latin for three years before beginning to study law. Like Gargan, Murphy read law with one of the founders of the Bar Association (Josiah G. Abbott) and graduated from Boston University Law School in 1876. Both men practiced alone throughout their careers.

Despite its hierarchy, lawyers in Boston after the Civil War became more socially diverse, particularly in the lower ranks of the profession. The liberal policies of admission and the rise of immigration combined to change the composition of the nineteenth-century bar in Boston. Overall, the size of the Boston bar increased from about 215 lawyers in 1840 to 301 in 1870. Only 61 of those 301 lawyers attended Harvard Law School, while most trained under less formal auspices. Less than half of them were actually born in Boston, and over a third came from outside of Massachusetts.

Few formal hurdles stood in the way of one seeking to become a lawyer in post-Civil War Boston. After 1836, when formal rules for admission were abolished, admission to the bar became haphazard at best. Typically, a prospective lawyer would study in a law office and, when ready, present himself to a judge for examination. The rigor and content of that exam depended on the mood or the dedication of that judge. The courts began requiring a written exam in 1855 but promptly dropped that requirement in 1859. In 1860, the courts gave applicants the option of three years legal study (in school or office) or an exam. That policy remained until 1876, when each applicant had to pass a bar examination. Fluctuating and informal admissions requirements thus made regulation of the bar difficult and entrance into the profession easy.

SIDNEY BARTLETT, WHO PRACTICED LAW FOR 69 YEARS, WAS THE LAST OF A GENERATION OF BOSTON ATTORNEYS LONG REMEMBERED AS LEADERS IN AMERICAN LAW AT LARGE. BY THE TIME OF HIS DEATH IN 1889, LEGAL PRACTICE AND THE GROWING NUMBER OF LAWYERS PRECLUDED ANY ONE ATTORNEY BEING ACKNOWLEDGED AS THE LEADER OF THE CITY'S BAR.

COURTESY, BOSTON BAR ASSOCIATION

Bar admissions were only part of the story. The civic context into which young Boston lawyers entered in the years after the Civil War was also changing. Nineteenth-century Bostonians understood legal training to be preparation for the assumption of a leadership role within the entire community. Boston lawyers, proud architects of the nation, saw their handiwork undone in the conflict over slavery. The Civil War shifted the spotlight away from lawyers and jurists and onto the politicians, soldiers, and businessmen who led the nation through the crisis. The failure of Radical Republicanism, led by Boston lawyer Charles Sumner, to rebuild the war-torn nation heightened the perception of decline. Young Boston attorneys Moorfield Storey and Samuel Hoar, both destined to play leading roles in Boston legal circles, witnessed this repudiation firsthand while working in Washington, D.C. In his later years, Storey wrote movingly of Sumner's futile efforts in the 1870s. Lawyers throughout America saw their public preeminence threatened by soldiers and politicians in these years. Nowhere was this perception more acute than in Boston, where lawyers gazed back upon more than a century of political, social, and intellectual leadership amongst their predecessors.

Comparisons of past and present led to diminished confidence in the legal profession around Boston. An after-dinner speaker in 1876 lamented that "no incomprehensible giants in the profession" remained. A local newspaper complained of the "shysters" who were invading the bar. In his memoirs, one local court officer recalled the alarming decline in the character of the bar during this period. Along with others, these voices made up a chorus of despair whose common refrain centered on declension within the legal community.

Just as the reputation of the bar and its leaders began to suffer after the Civil War, so, too, did the facade of unity among the profession. For one thing, by the 1870s, Boston's lawyers found it more and more difficult to agree upon the proper method of legal education. At Harvard, Dean Christopher Langdell introduced the case method of teaching, aiming to convey the scientific nature of the law to his students. Boston University established its own law school in 1872, expressly offering it as an alternative to Harvard. In this era, too, the first of the Irish immigrants who entered the city in the 1840s began to appear at the Yankee-dominated bar. Their presence served as another reminder of the changes occurring within the profession. By the mid 1870s, the lack of unanimity at the bar on various issues had begun receiving public notice. In at least one instance, the local press criticized the city's lawyers for their inability to speak in a common voice on issues of concern to the profession.

COURTESY, BOSTON PUBLIC LIBRARY, PRINT DEPARTMENT

Ashburton Place, as it appeared in the 1870s just before the school moved there from 36 Bromfield Street, was the home of Boston University Law School for several decades. Visible at the right center of this photo is the Greek Revival facade of 11 Ashburton, which the school occupied from 1895 on. Across the street was 8 Ashburton, the school's home from 1884 to 1895.

THE FOUNDING OF THE BAR ASSOCIATION OF THE CITY OF BOSTON

While the leading members of the bar in Boston met informally before the Civil War, a movement to revive the bar organization had begun by the end of the War. In 1866, a number of the city's leading lawyers, including

John C. Gray, John C. Ropes, and Oliver Wendell Holmes, Jr., formed the *American Law Review* in order to provide practicing lawyers with useful information. In one of its first issues, they called for the formation of a bar association in Boston to reverse the decline in influence and reputation of the lawyer in Boston. On the subject of appointments to legal offices, the Review noted the inability of the profession to sway those making decisions. "In more than one instance, the wishes of the profession have been used as an argument against the appointment

COURTESY, SOCIAL LAW LIBRARY, BOSTON

or election of the person it supported." Of the bar's diminishing prestige, the Review's authors had no doubt. "None of us desire to see our beloved profession degraded to a brokerage business," they asserted, "and yet we fear, and cannot conceal our fear, that such is the tendency of the age." The editors called for the formation of a bar association to bolster the status of Boston's lawyers.

The demand for a professional association grew. "It is the subject of constant remark at the bar," the Review reported of Boston, "that we need some kind of organization or association similar to those which exist in the medical profession." Lawyers saw a variety of associations for businessmen, doctors, laborers, and the clergy. But the bar could point only to a handful of clubs, boasting but a few members each, and devoted to social purposes only. In an era of associations, the absence of a lawyers' organization grew increasingly noticeable.

HERBERT L. HARDING WAS THE CO-COUNSEL SELECTED BY ROBERT MORSE TO ASSIST IN ARGUING AGAINST THE ADMISSION OF LELIA ROBINSON TO THE BAR IN 1881. THEIR BRIEF ADDRESSED NOT ONLY THE QUESTION AT HAND, BUT RELATED ISSUES SUCH AS WOMEN'S SUFFRAGE AS WELL AS WHETHER AND TO WHAT OFFICES WOMEN COULD BE ELECTED.

The benefits to be derived from such a legal society would aid in the restoration of the profession's standing and influence. Foremost, the new association would serve to police the bar. "It is time," the Review proclaimed, taking note of the bar's declining reputation, "that some measures were taken to expose and punish the malpractice of some unworthy members of our profession, who bring the law and lawyers into contempt." Further, the bar needed an active organization of lawyers to make its influence felt in the halls of the legislature. The proposed body would fulfill that need, thus restoring to the profession its time-honored role in the creation of law.

The leading lawyers of Boston drew inspiration from other cities in their plans to create a bar association. Undoubtedly, they were aware that the leading lawyers of New York City established the Association of the Bar of the City of New York in 1870. Much-publicized corruption among a judiciary tied to the Tweed Ring and the assault of a lawyer prompted that city's leading lawyers to organize. The New York Bar Association quickly gained a reputation for being a preserve of leading practitioners. Both their exclusive nature and their professed goals—to maintain "the honor and dignity of the profession," encouragement of social intercourse amongst the bar, and "promoting the administration of justice"—provided a model for bar organizations across the country.

Within eight years, leading lawyers organized bar associations in St. Louis, Cleveland, Chicago, and San Francisco, as well as Boston. In all, by 1878, lawyers around the country had formed sixteen new city and statewide associations. In the decades that followed, the number of bar associations around the country increased exponentially. In addition, a group of leading lawyers meeting in Saratoga Springs, New York, created a national organization, the American Bar Association. Several leading Boston lawyers were involved and through them Boston's bar maintained particularly close ties to the nationwide association for several decades.

In the winter of 1875, a private letter calling for the creation of a new bar association circulated among thirty-seven of Boston's most prominent lawyers. The exact origins of the letter are unclear, although Joseph A. Willard, Clerk of the Suffolk County Superior Court, later claimed to be the initiator of the note. He recalled that "for some time" he had felt the need for a bar association that would "elevate the tone of the bar and to look after cases of malfeasance." The original thirty-seven (and perhaps others) met on February 26, 1876, in the Superior Court Room. Sidney Bartlett, as the acknowledged leader of the bar, presided over the meeting to form the Bar Association of the City of Boston. The assembled lawyers appointed a Committee of Five, plus Sidney Bartlett and the meeting's Secretary, Albert Pillsbury, to prepare a plan for launching the Bar Association of the City of Boston.

COURTESY, SOCIAL LAW LIBRARY, BOSTON

That leaders from practice and politics lay behind the creation of the new Association is evident just from the composition of this seven-man committee. Aside from Bartlett, it included William Gaston, who had just completed a term as Governor two months earlier, the first Democrat to serve in twenty-three years. Previously, he had served as Mayor of Boston. The Speaker of the Massachusetts House of Representatives, John D. Long, also served on the organizing committee. Three years later, he began the first of three consecutive terms as Governor. Walbridge Field, another member, served for two years as Attorney General of the United States under President Grant. Five years later, he received an appointment to the Supreme Judicial Court of Massachusetts. The remaining members of the committee were highly respected lawyers, well-known within the legal community of Boston.

CHARLES R. TRAIN, FORMER ATTORNEY GENERAL OF MASSACHUSETTS, WAS APPOINTED BY CHIEF JUSTICE HORACE GRAY TO PRESENT THE ARGUMENTS OF LELIA ROBINSON REGARDING HER PETITION TO BE ADMITTED TO THE BAR. ROBINSON WROTE THE BRIEF, BUT BECAUSE SHE WAS NOT A MEMBER OF THE BAR, TRAIN HAD TO PRESENT IT TO THE COURT.

All thirty-seven founders of the Bar Association shared educational and cultural backgrounds. At least thirty-two of the thirty-seven attended college in an era when such an attainment remained uncommon, even among lawyers. Twenty-five of them had some connection to Harvard; eighteen attended as undergraduates while nineteen studied at Harvard Law School. Seven others attended Dartmouth College and the remainder attended either Colby, Middlebury, or Bowdoin. Twenty-six of them received at least part of their legal education in a law office—including sixteen of the nineteen Harvard Law students, the common practice prior to the Civil War.

These men were the products of an earlier era. All but six of them were over forty when they created the Association. Over half of them began to practice between 1820 and 1850 and thirty-one of the thirty-seven had been admitted to

COURTESY, SOCIAL LAW LIBRARY, BOSTON

the bar before the Civil War. Although their social backgrounds varied somewhat, nearly all of the men who launched the new Bar Association came of age professionally in a period when the profession was accustomed to playing a leading role in public affairs. Twenty of these thirty-seven men served at least one term in elective office. Five served on the bench at some point in their careers while two others accepted appointive office. These men were predominantly appellate lawyers; more than one-half of them appeared at least once before the Supreme Judicial Court in Suffolk County during 1875-76.

When the organizers held a meeting in May of 1876 for the "respectable members of the bar" to discuss their plans, they did not encounter universal approval. The *Boston Herald* reported "Considerable criticism of the movement" from members of the bar excluded from the meeting, whom the Herald reported were "large in numbers." They saw the movement as "a clique who desire to form a mutual admiration society, so exclusive that only those chosen from personal preferences will be admitted within the circle." "The founders," of course, "stonily disclaimed" any such intentions, responding that they wished only to expel those lawyers guilty of malpractice and "to bring together all those worthy of recognition." The issue of exclusivity, present from the start, would plague the Bar Association for more than half a century.

WILLIAM G. RUSSELL WAS A FOUNDER OF THE BOSTON BAR ASSOCIATION, PRESIDENT FROM 1882 TO 1884, AND ONE OF THOSE WHO ENVISIONED THE ORGANIZATION AS A GUARDIAN OF THE BAR, NOT MERELY IN TRACKING PROFESSIONAL ACTIVITIES, BUT IN ALL ASPECTS OF PRACTICE AND DISCIPLINE OF THOSE ADMITTED TO THE BAR.

But advancing professional standards and conduct was at the heart of the new Association. The second article of its new

Constitution sketched out the Association's basic goals: "The Association," it read, "is established to promote social intercourse among the members of the bar; to insure conformity to a high standard of professional duty; and to make the practice of the law efficient in the administration of justice." To accomplish its goals, the young organization elected Sidney Bartlett as its first President and established committees and by-laws. Most notably, they immediately employed a Judicial Committee (one of whose members was Oliver Wendell Holmes, Jr.) to monitor the conduct of the city's bar. They also insti-

tuted a nominating process which required that each applicant be recommended by two existing members, that the ten-member judicial committee approve all applicants, and the membership present at a regular meeting would vote to approve each new member. An annual dinner would be held to encourage a social spirit among members. Amendments to the Constitution frequently altered its rules, including a brief experiment with eliminating "intoxicating liquors" from the annual dinner, a move which was quickly repealed.

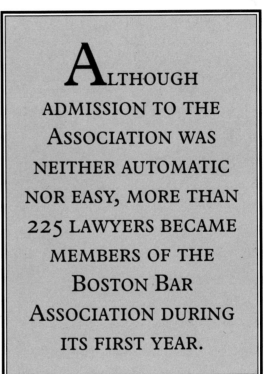

ALTHOUGH ADMISSION TO THE ASSOCIATION WAS NEITHER AUTOMATIC NOR EASY, MORE THAN 225 LAWYERS BECAME MEMBERS OF THE BOSTON BAR ASSOCIATION DURING ITS FIRST YEAR.

Although admission to the Association was neither automatic nor easy, more than 225 lawyers became members of the Boston Bar Association during its first year, a number that represented a clear majority of all lawyers then practicing in Suffolk County. In order to gain admission to the Association, candidates had to be recommended by two members, approved by the Judicial Committee and win at least four of every five votes cast by the members at a general meeting. Clearly, these hurdles were intended to make membership in the Association seem to be a privilege and to combat the perception that professional standards were slipping.

Immediately, the Bar Association decided that it would take on the responsibility of seeking the disbarment of all misbehaving lawyers in Boston, not just its own members, a step that even New York City's Bar Association hesitated to take. The Association made the investigation and initiation of grievance cases in court the responsibility of the Judicial Committee, thereby allowing just a few members the discretion to act as watchdogs for all of the city's lawyers. The early grievance policies and practices of the Association illustrate the ways in which it conceived of its role within the legal community of Boston: as the organized few governing the unorganized many.

Understanding itself in such terms, the fledgling Bar Association set out to make its influence felt in the profession. While it had no official standing from which to govern, the prominence of its members assured it power and influence. The growing concern about the quality of legal practitioners led to efforts to tighten the standards for entrance to the bar. In 1876, the same year Boston's leading lawyers created the Association, the Massachusetts Legislature raised standards for acceptance to the bar, requiring an exam of every applicant, regardless of the amount of formal study they had undertaken. The new law also established Bar Examiners for each county, to be appointed by the Supreme Judicial Court. The five lawyers appointed by the Court for Suffolk County were among the leading members of the Association. Members of the Bar Association, and in particular its leaders, dominated the Suffolk County Board through its twenty-one year existence as thirty of the thirty-five examiners who eventually served were members of the Association.

In late nineteenth-century America, women began to break down the barriers of discrimination which had previously prevented them from being accepted into the legal profession. The Association found itself directly involved in the efforts of women in Massachusetts to be admitted to practice law as Lelia J. Robinson, petitioned for admission to the bar. Robinson, graduating cum laude and fourth in her class at Boston University School of Law, found law school intellectually stimulating and devoid of discrimination. Had Robinson been a man, her application would have been routinely approved.

Rather, the Bar Examiners referred her application to Chief Justice Horace Gray, who asked the Association to submit a brief in opposition to Robinson's application. Ironically, Robinson's lawyer, former Attorney General and charter member of the Association, Charles R. Train, found himself opposing his own organization in court. Robert Morse, Jr., a member of the Executive Committee, and Herbert L. Harding represented the Association in the proceedings. They argued that women did not have the right to become attorneys, resting their argument on the narrow interpretation of the Fourteenth Amendment established in the Supreme Court's ruling in the Slaughterhouse Cases of 1873. Morse and Harding insisted that the right to become an attorney could only be granted by the state legislature. Robinson prepared her own briefs and urged the Court to view women as "citizens" in the broadest sense, contending that the 1876 licensing statute did not prohibit the admission of women.

In his opinion rejecting Robinson's petition, Chief Justice Gray agreed with Morse and Harding. But the General Court acted quickly in 1882, and made women eligible to practice law by statute. Lelia J. Robinson quickly passed the bar examination and was admitted to practice. Governor John D. Long, also a founder of the Bar Association and a strong supporter of women's rights, signed the bill into law.

Despite Robinson's victory, relatively few women practiced law in late nineteenth century Massachusetts, numbering forty-seven in 1900.

Despite its prominence in the Robinson case, the Association had great difficulty finding its public niche. Although the organization initially considered the creation a charitable arm, plans went nowhere. State and local leaders tended to call on the young organization to play a largely symbolic role. The primary formal public activity of the Bar Association in its first ten years appears to have been to advise on the question of the location of various courts or on their architectural features. For the most part, the newly-formed society lacked the tradition to act effectively as an organization on the public

The Boston Bar Association rented its first suite of rooms used as headquarters in the Federal Court-house, here shown newly built around 1885. Part of the rent was "paid" by allowing judges and other court officers to use the Association's library, housed in its suite.

Courtesy, Boston Public Library, Print Department

stage. The power of the Association stemmed from the actions of its leaders, not the organized impulse of the whole bar. The institutional character that did emerge for the Association was a product of the inherited patterns of thought and action of its organizers, not the result of a clear vision of the Association's public purposes.

REMAKING THE ASSOCIATION

MOORFIELD STOREY, BOSTON BAR ASSOCIATION PRESIDENT FROM 1909 TO 1913 AND LATER PRESIDENT OF THE NAACP, CAME OF AGE DURING THE CIVIL WAR AND ITS RECONSTRUCTION AFTERMATH. HARVARD-EDUCATED, HE WAS TYPICAL OF THE ASSOCIATION'S MEMBERSHIP AND LEADERSHIP WELL INTO THE TWENTIETH CENTURY, EVEN AS THE COMPOSITION OF THE BAR ITSELF WAS CHANGING.

COURTESY, SOCIAL LAW LIBRARY, BOSTON

Boston's lawyers quickly began to lose interest in the Association. By the early 1880s, attendance at Association meetings declined to the point that they often lacked the twenty-five members necessary for a quorum. According to one observer, the Association's inability to attract new members resulted from its having nothing to offer to most members of the profession. Nonmembers, this critic reported, "have either been indifferent toward it, or have congratulated themselves that they have no dues to pay and no annual dinners to eat."

Recognizing the waning of interest, Lauriston L. Scaife led a movement to reorganize the Association along more vigorous lines. In late 1883, Scaife, one of the younger members, moved that the Association appoint a committee to look into ways of "increasing the usefulness of this association." Scaife and several others formed that committee and over the ensuing year compiled a report outlining a thorough reorganization of the Association. The report unfavorably compared Boston's methods of proceeding with the work of bar associations in New York, Philadelphia, and London. The primary function of the Association, it concluded, had been to serve dinner once a year. Beyond an annual meal, the Association's formal accomplishments amounted to little. The dinner alone, they argued, was "hardly sufficient as the end aim or practical result of a general organization of the lawyers of Boston." The bar had a broader "duty" to police the profession and "to promote sound legislation."

Presented in 1885, the Scaife report proposed that the existing Judicial and Executive Committees be replaced by a Council of twenty-one members. That Council, along with a President, Vice President, Treasurer, and Secretary, would also serve on various committees of five to seven members, each responsible for a given task. A Committee on Admissions would take over the process of screening applicants to the Association. A Committee on Grievances would handle complaints of misconduct leveled at the members of the profession. An Executive Committee would deal with financial matters while the Library Committee looked after the library. Each Council member would serve a three year term, with seven being elected each year. The result of these changes, the reorganization committee hoped, would be more influence for the Association in each area, leading to greater interest in the Bar Association.

Beyond increased activism, the Scaife report proposed remaking the Bar Association in social terms as well. In late nineteenth-century Boston, the familiarity that lawyers and judges found by riding the circuit declined as increasing numbers of lawyers practiced only in the city. To foster greater social interaction

COURTESY, BOSTON BAR ASSOCIATION

among all members of the bar, Scaife's committee deemed it "essential" for the Association to establish quarters "where the members may meet familiarly." In this way, the bar could develop the esprit de corps and intimate knowledge of each other necessary for self-regulation. The days when lawyers could come naturally to know each other through daily interaction were gone, they report-

THE BUILDING OF A NEW COURTHOUSE FOR SUFFOLK COUNTY IN THE LATE NINE-TEENTH CENTURY SYMBOLIZED THE EXPANDING IMPORTANCE OF THE LAW IN BOSTON. COMPLETED IN 1886, THE "OLD COURTHOUSE" IS STILL IN SERVICE, DESPITE THE CONSTRUCTION OF THE "NEW COURTHOUSE," VISIBLE AT THE RIGHT, BUILT IN 1937.

ed. Social intercourse could no longer be taken for granted. It was necessary to take steps now to restore professional and social cohesion to the bar. The end result of the Scaife report was a more active bar association. The Association adopted the organizational changes suggested in 1885 by the Scaife committee but postponed indefinitely action on new quarters. Power within the Association became even more centralized in the new Council as it performed the "sole and entire management" of the Association. Through the various committees, Council members and officers conducted virtually all of the organization's busi-

ness. While the Association became more active, fewer members had access to power within the Association because the process of nominating officers and Council members was closed. Each year the Council appointed a nominating committee which proposed one person for each open Council spot, plus a single candidate for each office. The membership accepted or rejected that candidate, thereby minimizing competitive elections.

The composition of the Council over the next fifteen years reflected the limited access. Among the original Council and officers, all but three of the twenty-five members received at least one degree from Harvard. Subsequent Councils deviated little from that norm. The Council remained predominantly Yankee. The first Irish name, Charles Gallagher, did not appear on its rolls until 1888.

WILLIAM CALEB LORING, A FOUNDER OF THE BOSTON BAR ASSOCIATION, WAS ONE OF THOSE ATTORNEYS WHO USED THE ASSOCIATION TO PUSH FOR REFORM IN THE LEGAL SYSTEM. HE LATER SERVED AS FIRST PRESIDENT OF THE JUDICIARY COUNCIL, ONE OF THE MANY REFORMS THAT THE BOSTON BAR WAS INSTRUMENTAL IN ACHIEVING.

The only other Irishman to earn a spot on the Council before 1900 was Harvard-educated, erstwhile Congressman Patrick Collins, destined to become Mayor of Boston in 1900. In fact, from 1885 until 1900, the closed nomination system allowed only fifty-five men to serve on the twenty-one man Council. As the Association set out to become more active and influential, it also found itself a more centralized organization, as fewer members of the bar participated in its policy decisions.

The leaders of the Association set a more aggressive course over the next fifteen years, particularly with regard to the state of the profession in Boston. On a motion by founding member William G. Russell, the Association reiterated its policy that "proceeding against members of the bar should not be limited to cases within the professional acts of the attorney," thereby reasserting its right to stand in judgment of all members of the profession in Boston. Despite its lack of formal authority, the Association had sufficient influence to make its judgment effective. In 1889, attorney D. F. Crane still practiced law three years after the Association thought it had shut him down. As a result, the Bar Association convinced the legislature to pass a law providing for a $500 fine to be levied against any disbarred lawyer continuing to practice. Close relations between political leaders and the

COURTESY, BOSTON PUBLIC LIBRARY, PRINT DEPARTMENT

Association made it at times an informal arm of government. In one case, Boston Mayor Nathan Matthews, a member of the Bar Association, relied on the Association—not the police or another department of the city government—to undertake an investigation and to proceed against a local attorney who stood accused of attempting to intimidate city officials.

But the results of the Bar Association's cleanup efforts were mixed at best. Between 1886 and 1900, the Association succeeded in disbarring an average of less than two attorneys per year. That average remained steady despite a constant increase in the size of the bar in Boston. (By 1900, the number of lawyers practicing in Boston had roughly doubled since 1880.) The numbers of disbarred attorneys contradicted the Association's rhetoric about the decline in professionalism at the bar. Either the Association exaggerated the problems within the profession or its efforts to solve those problems proved ineffective.

After 1885, the organization began to speak up on a number of new fronts. The newly formed Committee on the Amendment of the Law proposed to make itself a clearinghouse on legal legislation, soliciting suggestions on the subject and lobbying at the state house for or against bills affecting the legal profession. Like reformers in other fields, the Association also began to demand expert, nonpartisan administration in place of the corrupt, ineffective machinery of party-run government. They advocated the revival of the appointed office of Solicitor General to replace the elected District Attorney. The Association offered similar advice with regard to the office of Register of Deeds. Other concerns for which the Bar Association sought reforms in this period included the quality of the judiciary and the need for an improved method of selecting juries. By the 1890s, cries for the reform of the legal system, and indeed for all aspects of public policy, arose in the press, on campaign trails, and in the halls of legislative bodies. The Association did not hesitate to add its voice to the chorus.

COURTESY, COMMONWEALTH OF MASSACHUSETTS, MASSACHUSETTS ART COMMISSION

WILLIAM GASTON WAS A FOUNDER OF THE ASSOCIATION IN 1876. HE WAS THEN SERVING AS GOVERNOR OF MASSACHUSETTS, BEGINNING A LONG TRADITION OF THE CONNECTION OF THE MODERN ASSOCIATION TO CITY AND STATE GOVERNMENT.

SEEKING LEGITIMACY: THE PROBLEM OF AN INTEREST GROUP

The question of whether the Association was the legitimate spokesman of the legal profession in Boston persisted. The bar in Boston continued to undergo profound changes. The Association did not. By one count, 1,472 men and women practiced law in and around Boston by 1900, triple the number of lawyers to be found in the city thirty years earlier. The rapid rise in the number of attorneys showed no sign of abating. Harvard and Boston University showed enrollments totaling 1,025 law students for the 1899-1900 school year. While not all of these students were destined to become lawyers in Boston, the supply of new lawyers did not dwindle. Between 1898 and 1900, 553 new lawyers passed the bar examination in Massachusetts.

This rapid influx of lawyers created not only a bigger bar, but a different one. The most obvious change involved the rise of the Irish. By 1889, at least 110 Irish Americans were practicing law in Boston, and several more occupied the bench. Following the Irish into the legal profession in Boston were immigrants of a variety of ethnic backgrounds, particularly Italians and German and Russian Jews. Women began to appear at the bar in this era, albeit in small numbers. By 1895, sixteen Boston women had followed in Lelia Robinson's footsteps to become practicing attorneys.

African-American attorneys had always been a part of Boston's bar, though relatively small in numbers. In 1861, E. J. Ruffin became the third black member of the Suffolk bar. In 1883, George L. Ruffin was named a judge of the Municipal Court of Charlestown by Governor Benjamin Butler.

While legal practitioners in Boston became more diverse, the leadership on the Association's Council continued to be drawn from Harvard or Harvard Law School. Just four attended the Boston University. Only two of the twenty-nine were of Irish descent. At the turn of the century, the Bar Association had 632 voting members, well under half the total number of lawyers at the bar in Boston. The social composition of those 632 did not resemble that of the whole bar. By that time, Irish-American lawyers made up nearly 20 percent of the lawyers in Boston but only 3 percent of the membership of the Association, a fact that did not escape the notice of Boston's Irish-American community. In demographic terms, the Bar Association and its leadership continued to become less and less like the legal profession in Boston.

In 1896, the Association centralized the powers of its Council, giving it more authority to initiate action without the prior approval of the whole membership. Burdened with a growing number of grievance cases and an expanding legislative load, Association leaders sought quicker and more practical ways to dispense with the Association's business. Previously, the Grievance Committee made its reports to the assembled members, who then voted to decide what steps would be taken. With the changes, the Council, without the consent of the members, could seek the disbarment of an accused attorney. The Council also took over the responsibility of deciding what proposed legislation to support or oppose on Beacon Hill. Although the regular meetings of the entire Association reserved the right to instruct the Council, in practice, even more power now rested in the hands of the fewer than thirty men serving on the Council. To some degree, most members welcomed the centralization of power in the Council. With busy practices, the members were less able to take part in the Association's activities as originally anticipated.

The extent of the members' participation emerged once again over the question of permanent headquarters. A report submitted in 1887 on the subject noted that "some of the younger members" thought that an established residence would attract new members and "develop the spirit of association, which we all believe to be one of the desirable features of a Bar Association." The same report insisted that the situation required "speedy action" in this area to maintain interest in the organization and to increase membership.

Not until 1897 did the Association seriously consider a plan to establish a permanent home. In fact it considered two plans to replace the borrowed courthouse rooms, one to rent and one to purchase rooms for Association offices. The principal requirement necessary to follow either plan was financial. The Association would need 600 members willing to pay twenty dollars in dues annually, a fifteen dollar increase.

Above all, advocates of new quarters for the Association sought to restore a sense of community to the bar in Boston. Recalling the arguments of Lauriston Scaife's committee in 1885, they pointed out that only a few of the leading lawyers in Boston enjoyed regular social and professional relations. In particular, the bar's "younger members" found themselves excluded from the goings-on within the more influential reaches of the profession. More-over, they argued, all members of the bar needed "equal facilities" in order to fulfill their professional obligation. In sum, the fundamental change that those in favor of a permanent headquarters for the Association hoped to bring about, was to make the Association "a more homogenous body than it is today." No longer could that homogeneity occur naturally, through the day-to-day interaction of a small, tight-knit bar.

Seekers of a building for the bar believed that the principal tool for professional unity was social intercourse. Pointing to the first clause in Article II of the Association Constitution, they argued that with the growing number of courts, lawyers, and laws, it was more and more difficult for them to exchange views. The bar needed a place where they could come together informally to discuss the legal issues of the day.

Both the bar and the Bar Association would benefit from a meeting place in another way, headquarters proponents claimed. Policing the bar required "a wide

COURTESY, BOSTON BAR ASSOCIATION

ALFRED HEMENWAY, BOSTON BAR ASSOCIATION FOUNDER AND PRESIDENT FROM 1905 TO 1909, ALSO SERVED AS PRESIDENT OF THE MASSACHUSETTS BAR ASSOCIATION AND AS VICE PRESIDENT OF THE AMERICAN BAR ASSOCIATION, EMBODYING THE CLOSE-KNIT WORLD OF NINETEENTH-CENTURY LEGAL PRACTICE. HEMENWAY WAS PRESIDENT WILLIAM MCKINLEY'S CHOICE FOR A SEAT ON THE U.S. SUPREME COURT. AFTER MCKINLEY'S ASSASSINATION, PRESIDENT THEODORE ROOSEVELT NAMED OLIVER WENDELL HOLMES INSTEAD.

acquaintance and plenty of opportunity for discussion, and for the dissemination of the news and facts relating to these matters." Since the leading practitioners rarely spent time in the lower courts, where, theoretically, most of the malpractice occurred, a center of social and professional activity for the bar would allow them to interact with ordinary practitioners. Thus armed with "an intimate knowledge of the characters and tendencies of the bar," the leaders of the Association would prove far more effective in cleaning up the profession in Boston.

Finally, supporters of permanent quarters believed, a broader bar meant a more effective bar. As new members joined, enticed by the added attraction of the Association's new home, the clout of the bar would expand. The debate over quarters became a debate over the public role of the Bar Association. Proponents sought to make the Association more representative of the profession and thus a more legitimate and effective voice of the bar.

COURTESY, BOSTON BAR ASSOCIATION

JOHN D. LONG, BOSTON BAR ASSOCIATION FOUNDER AND MASSACHUSETTS GOVERNOR, SUPPORTED WOMEN'S RIGHTS, AND SIGNED INTO LAW THE MEASURE THAT ALLOWED WOMEN TO PRACTICE LAW IN THE COMMONWEALTH.

Others in the Bar Association disagreed with both the goals and the methods of those desiring to change it. In an opposing report, a second committee claimed the Association had but two responsibilities. The first was to help the courts "in purging the bar of unworthy members and maintaining a high standard of professional character and conduct." The second was to furnish a library to assist lawyers, judges, and clients in their pursuit of the administration of justice. They believed the Association was already meeting these goals. To begin operating a social club would require a "radical change...in the character and objects" of the Association. Moreover, it would raise dues to such a level that it would more likely discourage membership than encourage it.

More importantly, opponents of the new quarters plan believed the Bar Association already represented Boston's legal profession. Their idea of representation differed from those seeking to widen membership. They considered the Association already to be acting as the arm of both "the whole profession and all that is best in it." An increased membership was unnecessary. Turning the Bar Association into a social club for lawyers of all ranks would only damage the organization's standing in the public mind, thereby reducing its influence. Their vision of what the bar should be harkened back to the founding of the Association. It was not the representative of the city's lawyers but rather the vehicle through which the best men of Boston's bar led the profession in their community.

The two competing visions of the Association's identity appeared to be the products of two generations. All of the five members of the committee reporting in favor of new quarters were born after 1850. They stressed the importance of attracting and maintaining the allegiance of younger attorneys. On the other side, three of the five opponents of the quarters plan were born before 1850 and had come of age professionally in the earlier era. Of the remaining two, one, A. Lawrence Lowell, was renowned for his conservative opinions. Not surprisingly, the elder members seemed more thoroughly wedded to the ideal of a hierarchical bar.

The Association put to a vote the question of whether it would represent primarily leading lawyers or be the voice of a more unified bar. The members overwhelmingly rejected the plan for new quarters. By a margin of 206 to 72, with 4 undecided and 322 not voting, the membership rejected the arguments of younger members seeking to broaden the character of the Association. Undoubtedly, the significant increase in dues cost the plan a great deal of support. But the Association's decision, nonetheless, reflected a certain understanding of how it was to represent the legal profession in Boston. The Association did not speak as the consensual voice of the entire bar but rather it represented the whole by expressing the views of the profession's best and most accomplished members, much like they believed the bar's best had done in the 1860s and before.

As the nineteenth century came to a close, the Association continued to cling to this older ideal. It remained faithful to a vision of a society and a profession marked by hierarchical leadership. But as a new generation established itself and the Association stepped up its public activity in the early twentieth century, the tension between an inherited institutional character and a changing social and professional environment placed limits on the power and influence of the Association.

COURTESY, BOSTON BAR ASSOCIATION

AUSTIN HALL WAS THE MAIN ACADEMIC BUILDING OF HARVARD LAW SCHOOL FOR DECADES. MOST BOSTON BAR ASSOCIATION MEMBERS WERE GRADUATES OF HARVARD LAW WELL INTO THE TWENTIETH CENTURY; LEADERS OF THE ASSOCIATION CAME ALMOST EXCLUSIVELY FROM HARVARD UNTIL EVEN LATER.

In the Public Interest

Reforming Society and the Bar, 1900–1930

IN THE NEW CENTURY, THE BAR Association of the City of Boston set out to remake a part of its community. Instead, the community remade the Bar Association.

After 1900, the Association steadily increased its efforts to reform the bar and the legal system in Boston. But burdened with its nineteenth-century legacy of organizational exclusivity, it found itself unable to keep up with a dynamic twentieth-century profession. As the Association ventured further into the public realm, its opponents questioned its motives and its legitimacy as a representative of the bar. Stung by these attacks and frustrated by its inability to accomplish the reforms it desired, the Association began to reconstitute itself in the 1920s. The organization that emerged differed from its nineteenth-century predecessor, both in its composition and in its perception of itself and the bar.

REFORMING SOCIETY

The social and political setting into which the Association thrust itself was a rapidly changing one. The emerging industrial-urban society transformed the practice of law, a process that began in the late nineteenth century. Lawyers at the top of the bar's hierarchy seized the opportunities generated by the new industrial and financial community. Boston lawyers pioneered in the establishment of entire new branches of the legal profession in response to industrial demands—patent law, corporate law, complex trust and estate planning, government regulation and tax law. These areas of law required different skills than those needed by the generalists who had led the bar in the early nineteenth century.

"The chief forum of the lawyer," proclaimed the *American Lawyer* in 1893, "has been transferred from the courthouse to the office. Litigation has declined, and counsel work has become the leading feature of practice." By the end of the nineteenth century, many lawyers shifted from solo practice and partnerships to the law firm. The rise of the law firm was a response to industrialization. The rate of growth in large firms—those with five or more members—paralleled the rise of business corporations. There were no large firms in Boston in 1882, but by 1904, there were

COURTESY, FRANK SITEMAN/BOSTON BAR ASSOCIATION

AT THE TURN OF THE CENTURY THE BOSTON BAR ASSOCIATION TOOK AN INCREASING ROLE IN LOBBYING THE STATE LEGISLATURE, A POLICY THAT CONTINUES TO THE PRESENT BENEATH THE GOLDEN DOME OF THE STATEHOUSE CAPITOL.

OPPOSITE: THE BOSTON BAR ASSOCIATION HELPED REMOVE MIDDLESEX COUNTY DISTRICT ATTORNEY NATHAN A. TUFTS FROM OFFICE FOR TAKING BRIBES. ALSO CONVICTED AND DISBARRED IN THE CASE WAS AN ATTORNEY LINKED TO MAYOR JAMES MICHAEL CURLEY.

COURTESY, BOSTON PUBLIC LIBRARY, PRINT DEPARTMENT

twelve. Lawyers working in large firms in Boston, New York and Chicago increased at an annual rate of 6.7 percent, while the total number of lawyers in these cities increased 1.7 percent. Not all large firms specialized in corporate law. Many listed themselves as engaged in general practice and relied upon the skill of individual practitioners within the firm. Still, the appearance of large firms changed the overall shape and outlook of the bar.

Louis D. Brandeis, who pioneered the successful large firm in Boston, saw both the advantages and disadvantages of a corporate practice. By offering knowledgeable business advice as well as legal counsel, Brandeis claimed that his clients were often able to avoid costly litigation. He also contended that a large firm offered the best chance for financial and professional success. When confronted by complaints from his young associates, whom he had hired from among Harvard Law School graduates, that he received all the credit for their work, Brandeis gave the young men a lesson in the realities of practicing in an industrial society. "The organization of large offices," said Brandeis in 1896, "is becoming more and more a business—and hence also a professional necessity—if properly planned and administered—it must result in the greatest efficiency to clients and the greatest success to the individual members [of the firm] both pecuniary and in reputation."

While he defended the large firm and the rewards that came from the practice of corporate law, Brandeis and a handful of others were troubled by the alliance between big business and lawyers. Brandeis's partner, George R. Nutter, bemoaned the long-term effects of this relationship. For the "men higher up at the bar," Nutter told Brandeis, the practice of law had changed since 1880 "from the determination of rights in court to advising and taking part in business enterprises." The result was, continued Nutter, that "while business standards may have improved a good deal, I think that the legal standards, by contact with them, have deteriorated somewhat." Nutter concluded that all "lawyers to a considerable extent become not persons whose advice is followed, but persons hired to carry through what their employers want to have done. One purchases legal brains now in the same way as he purchases industrial labor or anything else."

By the early twentieth century, the consequences of the nation's unprecedented industrial expansion after the Civil War became clear. Levels of urban poverty reached unprecedented heights and the flocks of recent immigrants from Eastern Europe gave city slums a more alien aura. An economic downturn in the 1890s spurred unrest among farmers and laborers. At the same time, the American economy changed in bewildering new ways, as large trusts and corpo-

COURTESY, SUPREME JUDICIAL COURT

rations emerged. Fueled by an explosion in the popular media, a new sense of urgency in American public life emerged in the first two decades of the twentieth century.

This sense of urgency led Americans to seek remedies for their ills in a multitude of ways. Many sought to alleviate poverty, Americanize immigrants and restore the moral fiber of the nation's urban poor. Others pointed to the growing interdependence of urban and industrial society and advocated greater government activism in the field of social welfare. Still others sought through regulation to curb corporate excess or to ensure that big business served the public interest efficiently. Reformers of yet another

THOUGH LONG ESTABLISHED AS THE PREDOMINANT COURT OF THE COMMONWEALTH, THE SUPREME JUDICIAL COURT AT THE TURN OF THE CENTURY RETAINED SOME OF THE OLD INFORMALITY: THE JUSTICES DID NOT WEAR ROBES, A PRACTICE ADOPTED ONLY LATER.

stripe focused on reforming the political realm, attempting to root out corruption and replace partisan politics with scientific, expert-led governance.

The Bar Association waded into this welter of reform during the first two decades of the twentieth century. It began its attempts to reform the profession and the legal system by trying to influence the lawmaking process. In 1904, the Association instructed its Committee on the Amendment of the Law to begin "systematic scrutiny" of the burgeoning output of the state legislature on legal matters, authorizing the committee to represent the Association in legislative hearings on a regular basis. The goal was a "more active approach" to lawmaking, one that ensured that the Association's interests were represented in the legislative process. Within a few years, the legislature's Joint Judiciary Committee, which dealt with legal legislation, regularly referred bills of interest to the Association for comment, thus providing the Association with significant say in which measures were introduced on the floor of the legislature.

COURTESY, BOSTON PUBLIC LIBRARY, PRINT DEPARTMENT

BY THE 1890S THE CENTER OF BOSTON'S LEGAL SCENE HAD BEGUN TO SHIFT TOWARD STATE AND FEDERAL STREETS. BUSY STATE STREET WAS CAPTURED IN THIS RARE PHOTOGRAPH JUST BEFORE THE TROLLEY LINES WERE PUT IN. NOTE THE MEN IN FORMAL DRESS AND TOPHATS, PERHAPS ATTORNEYS, ON THE SIDEWALK.

The Association typically endorsed legislative proposals which reflected the conservative reformism that had long characterized the organization. It continued to advocate appointment rather than election for sheriffs, district attorneys and court officers. Whenever possible, the Association preferred that power rest with an appointed judiciary rather than with the public or its elected officials. It repeatedly supported attempts to give the courts, particularly the Supreme

Judicial Court, the power to control admission to the bar, juror selection and the appointment of court officers. The Association strongly opposed the growing cry after 1910 for the popular election of judges.

Because a considerable amount of power rested with the bench, the Bar Association focused a great deal of its efforts on the quality of the courts and judiciary. Although its leaders often informally advised the governor on prospective nominees for the Massachusetts bench, in 1914, the Bar Association established a "Standing Committee on Vacancies in Judicial and Other Court Offices," which, three years later, became a permanent "Committee on the Administration of Justice." Given broad responsibilities, this committee was to "consider the efficiency of the judicial system and the registries, and all vacancies in and appointments to judicial office, and all other offices of the courts," to recommend changes in the courts and court offices and to report on the workload of Suffolk County's courts.

The influence of the Association increased when Massachusetts formed a special body charged with overseeing court reform. In response to rising criticism of the judicial system, Governor Calvin Coolidge appointed a three-person "Judicature Commission" in 1919, instructing it to recommend methods of alleviating the problems of the judicial system. In 1924, the legislature adopted the principal proposal of the Commission, establishing a permanent Judicial Council that would act as an advisory body on legal reform. To a large degree, the new Council was a child of the Bar Association. Two of the three members of the Commission who recommended its creation, former Supreme Judicial Court Justice Henry N. Sheldon and George R. Nutter, were longtime members of the Association. The first president of the Judicial Council, William C. Loring, was a founding member of the Association. Frank W. Grinnell, the Council's secretary, was a member of Boston's Bar Association and secretary of the Massachusetts Bar Association. The creation of the Judicial Council provided the Association with a sympathetic official ear for its complaints about the ills of the state's legal apparatus.

The Bar Association also sought to improve the judicial system by making it more available to all citizens. In 1900, a number of leading lawyers "closely identified with the Bar Association" established the Boston Legal Aid Society. They included Lewis S. Dabney, then president of the Association, Moorfield Storey and several other officers and Council members. The main reason for the exis-

> BECAUSE A CONSIDERABLE AMOUNT OF POWER RESTED WITH THE BENCH, THE BAR ASSOCIATION FOCUSED A GREAT DEAL OF ITS EFFORTS ON THE QUALITY OF THE COURTS AND JUDICIARY.

tence of the society was to provide legal representation for impoverished clients. The Society took only those clients whose cases it judged worthy, charging them a small fee. A privately funded and privately run operation, the Boston Legal Aid Society initially received the bulk of its support from nonlawyers.

The four to seven lawyers who staffed the Legal Aid Society were imbued with the progressive ideals of Dean Roscoe Pound of Harvard Law School. The staff attorneys became quite busy; in 1916, they handled 2,300 cases, of which only about 9 percent went to court. Most of their work involved wages and domestic relations.

Although the Association did not officially create the Legal Aid Society, the two organizations maintained close ties. By 1916, informal cooperation resulted in a formal relationship. The Legal Aid Society began to act as "an official investigative arm" of the Association, reporting on misconduct at the bar in the lower reaches of the profession. In turn, the Bar Association began providing the society with financial assistance. During World War I, the two institutions cooperated on several fronts, offering free legal assistance to families of military personnel and maintaining for free the clientele of attorneys serving overseas until their return.

COURTESY, SOCIAL LAW LIBRARY, BOSTON

HOLLIS R. BAILEY, BOSTON BAR ASSO-CIATION MEMBER AND CHAIRMAN OF THE BOARD OF BAR EXAMINERS, WROTE AN INFLUENTIAL STUDY OF BAR ADMISSIONS IN 1907 THAT RECOMMENDED HIGHER STAN-DARDS, A STANCE FREQUENTLY TAKEN BY THE ASSOCIATION. HIS RECOMMENDATION FOR A UNIFIED BAR ORGANIZATION, HOWEVER, WAS NEVER ACCEPTED BY THE ASSOCIATION.

Urging its members to support legal aid, Bar Association leaders insisted that "both individual attorneys and this Association, representing the body of the Boston bar, are under obligation to the society." They believed that "the simplest and most economical" way to fulfill this responsibility was to assist the Legal Aid Society in its efforts to serve the poor. Smith, in his 1918 report to the society, reminded his readers of the importance of legal aid: "If democracy means anything it must include justice as the right of every citizen."

With the publication in 1919 of Reginald Heber Smith's book on legal aid, entitled *Justice and the Poor*, the Boston Legal Aid Society's voluntaristic approach to legal services became a national model. Smith, a 1914 graduate of Harvard Law School, began his legal career as a staff attorney for the society. Drawing on his experiences at the society, he wrote *Justice and the Poor*, a book which swiftly earned widespread notice within the profession. Smith became the leading expert on the subject of legal aid, both locally and nationally, and the Boston model became a dominant one. His prominence thrust him into a leading role within the Boston bar, where he both practiced privately and advised on legal aid issues.

The basic problem, as outlined in *Justice and the Poor*, was the inability of poor people to gain access to respectable legal representation. Unable to afford reputable attorneys and, in the case of immigrants, unfamiliar with the legal system, the urban poor became the prey of unscrupulous practitioners. From this situation sprang the legal profession's declining reputation. Given this set of circumstances, the leaders of Boston's bar believed the Legal Aid Society served not only to assist underprivileged clients, but to help rid the profession of its worst elements. Importantly, the proposed remedy of the Legal Aid Society sought neither to alter radically the law nor to change the legal system. Rather, like so many undertakings by the leaders of the Boston bar, it was designed to return the administration of justice to respected lawyers in Boston.

THE BOSTON BAR AND THE MASSACHUSETTS BAR ASSOCIATION

Since it pinned so much of its reform hopes on the respectable elements of the bar, the Association continued its efforts to maintain the purity of the profession. As the bar in Massachusetts continued to expand, the Association gradually stepped up its efforts to prosecute dishonest attorneys. But simply policing the city's bar was not enough. As attorneys trained in all regions of the Commonwealth descended on Boston, the need for consistent standards of admission to the bar grew more evident. In 1897, Massachusetts established a statewide Board of Bar Examiners to ensure uniform requirements for entrance to the bar, particularly in the counties outside Boston. As the bar grew and the flow of lawyers in and out of Boston increased, monitoring the bar required greater efforts.

But the establishment of a state bar association did not follow directly on the heels of the State Board of Bar Examiners. As Frank Grinnell later recalled, interest in cooperation with outlying bar associations was "rather lukewarm." As early as 1900, the Association sought to develop a cooperative relationship with other bar associations in the state in an attempt to exert greater influence over legislation. Over the next decade, pressure to establish a state organization mounted. Yet a state bar came about slowly; in 1905, the Bar Association rejected a plea to launch a state bar association. In 1907, Hollis Bailey, an Association member as well as the chairman of the state's Board of Bar Examiners, published a historical study of bar admission practices, concluding that contemporary requirements were too lax and calling for greater attention to admission standards for the entire Commonwealth. Echoing similar views of the American Bar Association, he advocated formation of a statewide organization to accomplish

COURTESY, BOSTON PUBLIC LIBRARY, PRINT DEPARTMENT

GLEASON L. ARCHER, WHO FOUNDED THE SUFFOLK UNIVERSITY SCHOOL OF LAW IN HIS LIVING ROOM, CLASHED WITH THE BOSTON BAR ASSOCIATION OVER ACCREDITATION OF HIS SCHOOL IN THE 1910S. BY 1938, WHEN THIS PICTURE WAS TAKEN, HE WAS PRESIDENT OF SUFFOLK UNIVERSITY AND SUFFOLK LAW SCHOOL GRADUATES WERE JOINING THE ASSOCIATION.

that goal. Despite the continued urgings of Bailey and others, Boston's bar offered no official endorsement of a formalized state bar association.

When the Massachusetts Bar Association finally came into being in 1909, it looked peculiarly like an arm of the Bar Association of the City of Boston. Organized in Boston, nearly two-thirds of its original members practiced in the city. The second and fourth of its first seven presidents were members of the Association. Three of them had already served as Association presidents and the fourth was an original member of the Boston organization. Ten of the original twenty-one Executive Committee members of the new organization were also members of Boston's Bar Association. Frank Grinnell, who later served as secretary of the Massachusetts Bar Association from 1915 to 1960, had joined Boston's Bar Association in 1899. Given the many links between the two groups, cooperation characterized relations between them in most areas from the outset. A close relationship between Grinnell and George Nutter, who served on the Association's Council from 1914 to 1927 and as its president from 1923 to 1927, was just one of the ties that ensured cohesive action by the two groups in efforts to raise admission standards to the bar, the establishment of the Judicial Council and the creation and publication of a code of ethics for the bar.

COURTESY, HARVARD LAW SCHOOL ART COLLECTION

Despite the close ties between the leaders of the Association and the new Massachusetts Bar Association, inevitable differences of opinion arose between the two groups, particularly over bar discipline. Initially, the Massachusetts Bar Association authorized its Grievance Committee to pursue complaints against only those attorneys outside Boston. Yet that committee was composed largely of Boston attorneys. Eleven of the original fifteen members belonged to Boston's Bar Association, by far the largest percentage of Association members on any committee of the new organization. Initially, the new state bar association afforded Boston lawyers control of the grievance process for the whole state. Attorneys and local bar associations in other parts of the state complained of the independence given the Boston association but denied to them. Although jurisdictional disputes between the two organizations increased, the Boston bar continued to control the grievance process in its own community and to exert great influence on outlying areas through the state association. Far from creating a competitor to Boston's Bar Association, the establishment of the Massachusetts Bar Association provided

WILLIAM H. LEWIS, SON OF FORMER SLAVES, GRADUATE OF AMHERST COLLEGE AND HARVARD LAW, WAS THE FIRST AFRICAN-AMERICAN TO BECOME A MEMBER OF THE BOSTON BAR ASSOCIATION (1915). HE HAD ALREADY COMPILED A DISTINGUISHED PUBLIC SERVICE RECORD, INCLUDING AN APPOINTMENT AS ASSISTANT U.S. ATTORNEY GENERAL, THE FIRST BLACK TO SERVE ON ANY SUB-CABINET POST IN U.S. HISTORY (1911–1913).

the leaders of Boston's Bar Association with the opportunity to widen their influence over the profession.

REFORMING THE PROFESSION

Boston's Bar Association accomplished little of what it hoped in the way of professional reform. The continued growth and diversification of the bar outpaced the ability to ride herd on it. While the Association demanded tougher admission standards, the legislature weakened them. Though the Association pursued its prosecution of grievances with increasing vigor, it had little to show in the way of results. A similar story could be told for the Association's attempts to influence legislation. The leaders of Boston's bar, finding themselves unable to effect the changes in public policy they sought, could feel their influence wane.

Reforming the legal profession meant keeping up with it—no easy task. By 1910, Boston had three new law schools. In 1898, the YMCA established a law school (which would become Northeastern University's law school), relying initially on Harvard professors and practitioners such as Louis D. Brandeis. In 1906, Gleason Archer, lawyer and entrepreneur, began teaching law in his Roxbury living room. His Suffolk Evening Law School awarded law degrees within a decade. In 1908, Arthur W. MacLean, law partner of Gleason Archer, opened the Portia Law School, forerunner of the New England School of Law, and offered the first all-women's law school in Boston. With the opening of these three institutions, the avenue leading into Boston's legal profession became significantly wider.

The three new law schools, which appealed to the middle and working classes, immigrants and women, fueled the growth of the profession in the Boston area. Between 1900 and 1905, the Commonwealth minted an average of over 250 new lawyers each year, more than half of whom pursued their careers in Boston. The new law schools substantially increased this total. In 1915, the first year in which it granted degrees, the Suffolk law school had 460 students. Thirteen years later, it boasted 4,000 students, most of them destined to practice locally. In 1926 alone, Portia trained 436 women to be lawyers. In addition, the YMCA law school and its more established counterparts continued to provide their share of the lawyers entering the city. The result was a burgeoning bar. In 1900, 1,472 lawyers practiced in the Boston area. By 1920, that number had grown to 2,560. A decade later, it ballooned to 4,000 aided in part by the opening of nearby Boston College Law School.

Among the many new lawyers were women and immigrants. In 1905, nineteen women practiced law in Boston. By 1920, that number had reached 103 and was climbing. Of the 1,311 lawyers in Boston in 1905, at least 550 were immigrants or descendants of immigrants. Most came from Irish stock; Jews and Italians predominated among the remainder. Between 1920 and 1930, the number of foreign-born lawyers in Massachusetts rose 80 percent, due in large measure to the availability of schools like Suffolk, Portia and the YMCA School. A smaller number of African-Americans had law practices as well. These developments reflected a steadily increasing heterogeneity of the bar in Boston.

For the leaders of the Association, this great influx of lawyers signaled anything but a healthy profession. Lamenting the declining character of the bar, the leaders of the Association sought to impose higher educational standards for lawyers. Hollis Bailey, reflecting a national concern, pointed out that "Massachusetts is behind many of the states in its standards of admission to the bar.... Some applicants are recommended who have much less than a high school training." As Alfred Z. Reed pointed out in his national survey of legal education in 1921, acceptance standards of law schools were extremely diverse, with leading schools like Harvard requiring a college degree and evening law schools like Suffolk and Portia barely requiring a high school diploma. Only ten states even made a high school degree necessary for admission entrance into the profession. Over the first three decades of the twentieth century, no issue would occupy the Association's energy so much as raising the requirements for admission to the bar.

Their crusade for stiffer entrance standards led them into a political minefield. Although the Board of Bar Examiners had pressed for stricter rules of admission since 1904, it was not until 1910 that they succeeded in securing approval from the Supreme Judicial Court for requiring either a high school diploma or its equivalent. The court delayed implementation of the new rules until 1914 in order for those without a high school education who were seeking admission to finish their preparation and join the bar. Capitalizing on the delay, opponents of the change mobilized against the revised requirements.

Martin Lomasney led the legislative charge against the tougher rules. Lomasney, political boss of Boston's West End since the 1880s, represented a district full of first- and second-generation Italian and Jewish immigrants. The expanding profession of the law, accessible through institutions like Suffolk law school, represented one of the few ways for his constituents to climb the professional ladder. For West Enders, and

VERSES AND SONGS

MY FEMININE ATTORNEY

Air: *Little Annie Rooney*

A sentimental rhymester I;
(My verse the public will not buy).
But yet for her I madly sigh,
  My feminine attorney.
Her soul is set on other pleas
Than those I proffer on my knees;
My suit is one that brings no fees,—
  My feminine attorney.

CHORUS:

  She's my sovereign,— I'm her slave;
  She's an angel,— I'm a knave.
  But she won't marry; thinks, on the whole,
  A feminine attorney should be a *feme sole.*

I study sonnets by the score,
To ladies whom the bards adore;
I cast their garnered wealth before
  My feminine attorney.
She only says, "The fellow dotes;
The raving rhapsodies he quotes
Have not the charm of Crocker's Notes,"
  My feminine attorney.

CHORUS.

COURTESY, BOSTON BAR ASSOCIATION

NINE YEARS AFTER WOMEN RECEIVED THE RIGHT TO BECOME ATTORNEYS IN MASSACHUSETTS, THE MALE-DOMINATED BAR STILL HAD ITS RESERVATIONS, AS ILLUSTRATED BY THE LYRICS OF THIS 1912 SONG FOR THE ALL-MALE ABSTRACT CLUB. SIMILAR SENTIMENTS ATTENDED EFFORTS TO ADMIT WOMEN TO THE BOSTON BAR ASSOCIATION.

others like them, the movement to raise the standards of admission to the bar represented "discrimination against the Jew, the Italian, the same kind of discrimination that the Irish were subjected to fifty years ago."

Despite its fervent lobbying, the Association lost the battle to tighten bar admission requirements. Although it "strenuously opposed" eight different bills designed to undo the steps taken by the Board of Bar Examiners and the Supreme Judicial Court, it failed to prevent Lomasney and his political allies from requiring two years of study in any high school, day or evening, in order to take the bar exam. An applicant needed neither a diploma nor a passing mark on an equivalency exam.

The defeat marked the beginning of twenty years of frustration for the Association on the subject of bar entry rules. It continued to fight for higher standards, but a decade later the Association still complained that "so many insufficiently trained men have appeared at the bar in recent years that the general level of training and character of Massachusetts lawyers seems to be getting constantly lower." The legislature repeatedly rejected the organization's overtures to allow the courts to control bar admissions. Alternative strategies that relied on the Association to screen applicants itself went nowhere because, as George Nutter noted, "a private association seemed to have no way to compel candidates to submit to the examination." Acknowledging failure in 1927, the Association admitted that, after a dozen years of trying, it had only "the dull drab of non-accomplishment" to show for its extensive efforts.

COURTESY, BOSTON PUBLIC LIBRARY, PRINT DEPARTMENT

MARTIN M. LOMASNEY, THE "MAHATMA" OF BOSTON'S DEMOCRATIC PARTY, WAS A LEADER IN THE MOVEMENT TO KEEP THE BOSTON BAR ASSOCIATION AND ITS ALLIES FROM INCREASING THE REQUIREMENTS FOR BECOMING AN ATTORNEY.

The Bar Association was no more able to chase unethical attorneys out of the profession than they were able to keep unqualified ones from getting in. Invariably, the organization praised the work of its Grievance Committee in ridding the bar of dishonest lawyers. But a glance at the numbers suggests the Association never accomplished as much as it thought it did. From 1900 to 1920, it instituted approximately four disbarment proceedings per year, up from its average of two per year in the late nineteenth century. At the same time, the number of complaints about lawyers received by the Association doubled. In the ensuing ten years, the rate of complaints received by the Association skyrocketed. In 1930, the Association's grievance committee entertained 681 reports of misbehavior, ten times more than it had in 1913. That same year, however, it instituted just six disbarment proceedings and handed out another half-dozen reprimands. With every passing year, an overburdened Grievance Committee proved less and less able to monitor the profession.

The Bar Association had little in the way of tools to pursue the many complaints against attorneys. More often than not, the secretary of the Grievance Committee handled the complaint himself, either mediating the dispute or deciding to dismiss it altogether. When the Association did pursue a case, it often languished for months or years on the docket of the backlogged Grievance Committee. The Association possessed no official authority to compel testimony. Nor were its findings or reports admissible in court. Although the Attorney General's office assumed the responsibility of prosecuting disbarments or assigning private attorneys to such cases in 1919, it usually did so at the request of a bar association. The responsibility fell back on the shoulders of the bar associations in 1924, when the legislature repealed the earlier law that had centralized the prosecution of disbarments with the Attorney General.

Before long, the Association came under fire for its inability to police the legal profession. In 1929, Attorney General Joseph Warner reported to the legislature that bar associations in Massachusetts had failed to monitor the bar adequately. "The present method of proceedings instituted by the bar associations have proven inefficient and ineffectual," Warner concluded, adding that "very few proceedings are commenced and actions which are commenced drag indefinitely." The Judicial Council backed up Warner, noting that the lack of official authority resting with bar associations prevented them from being effective. Though the Association issued a statement of protest, even the local press concluded that Boston's Bar Association and its sister organizations had proven themselves incapable of cleaning up the expanding profession.

COURTESY, BOSTON BAR ASSOCIATION

Louis Brandeis was a famous attorney by the time of his nomination to the U.S. Supreme Court in 1916, but his attacks on attorney greed and exploitation, as well as his Jewish identity, left many Boston attorneys cool towards him. Others spoke for him, however, indicating the growing range of attitudes toward legal philosophy within the city's bar.

In other areas, the Association encountered the same difficulty. Keeping up with the plethora of laws emanating from the state house proved as difficult as keeping up with the growth in the number of lawyers. The crisis of the new century provoked a storm of legislation seeking to resolve the problems of modernizing society. Many leaders of the bar viewed much of this "overlegislation" as either incompetent or irresponsible. They feared the law was becoming a tangled, incoherent collection of overlapping and contradictory rules. The Association's attempt to stem this flow, or at least direct it, through the stepped-up activity of its Committee on the Amendment of the Law met with limited success. It found itself overwhelmed by a flood of proposed laws. In 1914, the Association's legislation committee studied 127 legislative matters and actively opposed or supported forty-four of them. Four years later, the same committee considered over 300 potential laws yet acted on only thirty-six. Seven volunteers proved increasingly inadequate to the task of monitoring the feverish pace of lawmaking in an urbanizing, industrializing community.

PROBLEMS IN THE PUBLIC SPHERE

If the rapid growth and change of the early twentieth century left the Association breathless, the politics of the period left it stymied. Even when successful, the Yankee-tinged character of the Association made it a lightning rod for attacks launched by Boston's ethnic politicians. For the Bar Association of the City of Boston, the pursuit of the politics of reform led it quickly and inevitably into the swampy politics of ethnic antagonism.

Pinanski, Abraham E., S.		1910	1913
101 Milk St.			
Pinkham, Walter S., S.		1890	1894
Old South Bldg.			
Power, Clara Louise, S.		1895	1916
Probate Court.			
Powers, Samuel L., W.		1875	1885

COURTESY, BOSTON BAR ASSOCIATION

IT TOOK 15 YEARS FOR CLARA POWER TO BE ADMITTED TO THE ASSOCIATION, BUT IN 1916 SHE FINALLY BROKE THE GENDER BARRIER. AS HER LISTING ON THE MEMBERSHIP ROLLS INDICATES, SHE WAS A CLERK IN SUFFOLK PROBATE COURT, AND THUS PROBABLY A SAFE CHOICE AS THE FIRST WOMAN TO BE MADE A MEMBER.

Strangely, a moment that should have filled the Boston bar with pride—the nomination of one of its own to the United States Supreme Court—found both the bar and the Bar Association split. President Woodrow Wilson's selection of Louis D. Brandeis to sit on the Supreme Court of the United States met with strident opposition from some members of the Boston bar. Although a divided Association did not take an official position, the actions of several of its leading members, who claimed to be speaking for the lawyers of Boston, damaged the reputation of the Association and created tension within it. Supporters of Brandeis among Boston's attorneys rallied to his cause, offering testimony on his behalf in the U.S. Senate and ultimately helping him to a seat on the nation's highest court.

Brandeis's politics made him controversial within the Boston bar. By 1916, Brandeis had established a national reputation as a crusader and a critic of the legal profession and of corporate America. Publications like *Other People's Money*, a vitriolic attack on large business enterprises, thrust Brandeis's name into the public eye. He held his own colleagues largely responsible for many social ills, attacking what he saw as an alliance between top lawyers and greedy big business, proclaiming that "we hear much of the 'corporation lawyer,' and far too little of the 'people's lawyer.'"

Conservative lawyers mobilized to thwart the Brandeis nomination. A group of lawyers and businessmen from Boston obtained fifty-five signatures on a petition attacking Brandeis's reputation, claiming he lacked "judicial temperament and capacity" and "the confidence of the people." At the Senate confirmation hearings, a number of prominent Bar Association members, including Edward W. Hutchins, Moorfield Storey and Hollis Bailey, criticized Brandeis's "general reputation" among members of the bar. Storey portrayed Brandeis as unethical, accusing him of deceptive tactics in a number of cases. Hollis Bailey acknowledged the nominee's legal ability but labeled him "not entirely trustworthy." But George Nutter supported Brandeis, his law partner, as did George Anderson, a Bar member who represented Brandeis at his Senate confirmation hearings and who questioned those who testified against him.

The opposition to Brandeis failed, but it laid bare the divisions within the Boston bar. Sherman Whipple, another prominent Boston attorney, pointed to key reasons for the resistance to the appointment of Brandeis. "He has antagonized, by an attempt to carry out his ideas, very important and powerful interests," Whipple explained, adding that "the feeling of bitterness toward him is something which is very unpleasant to contemplate." Whipple also noted that Brandeis's personal relations with other lawyers were not the smoothest. "If he had been different, had not so held aloof, had mingled more with the Bar, discussed more doubtful points with other lawyers, they would not have misjudged him." Beneath it all, George Nutter, one of Brandeis's law partners, detected yet another source of antagonism toward the nominee: "the distilled essence of anti-Semitism." Such a charge rings true amid the consistent efforts of Brandeis's opponents to paint him as an unscrupulous, conniving legal advocate.

Although the Association refrained from taking any formal position on the nomination of its longtime member, prominent members played key roles on both sides of the fight. The result was a period of internal uneasiness for the Association, as members eyed each other suspiciously at meetings and opponents scurried to mend fences in the aftermath.

Another public issue affecting the Association was the struggle of the Suffolk Law School to gain accreditation from the state. In 1912, six years after it opened, Gleason Archer's school sought from the state legislature a charter permitting it to grant law degrees. The bill giving Suffolk degree-granting powers passed the House and Senate twice only to have it vetoed by Governor Foss each time. Finally,

COURTESY, BOSTON PUBLIC LIBRARY, PRINT DEPARTMENT

Henry L. Shattuck, squarely planted in the Brahmin, Republican traditions of the Boston bar, nonetheless led the way in 1917 by proposing that elections to the Association's all-important Council be opened to competition among candidates.

on its third passage, David I. Walsh, the Commonwealth's first Irish Catholic governor, signed the bill into law, thereby dramatically expanding the number of lawyers in Boston.

In 1921 and 1922, the Bar Association succeeded in achieving the removal from office of two corrupt district attorneys, their disbarment and the disbarment of their chief co-conspirator. While this accomplishment earned the Association great praise, it also had to endure a firestorm of public invective in its wake. Like so many public issues of that day in Boston, it turned into a battle waged along class and ethnic lines.

At least as far back as the 1880s, Irish Americans dominated Boston's population. But their political dominance of the city did not follow automatically from their numerical superiority. For a time, Irish and Yankee politicians ruled the city together in a fragile coalition. But by the 1910s, that cooperation had disintegrated, succeeded by a politics of ethnic and class antagonism. The foremost practitioner of this new style of politics was James Michael Curley, elected mayor in 1914. Curley's campaigns featured outrageous insults directed at the city's Puritan heritage and its political reformers. In turn, he faced vociferous attacks from the Good Government Association, the Yankee-dominated reform organization seeking better government. The leader of the Good Government Association during the 1920s, George Nutter, was also perhaps the leading member of the Bar Association. With the well-known Nutter at the helm, the Bar Association could not help but assume a clear political identity. Joseph Pelletier, of French and Irish extraction, served several terms as the District Attorney of the Suffolk County before allegations surfaced that he received money in exchange for killing certain prosecutions. A well-known political figure, he also occupied a prominent position within the Knights of Columbus, a Catholic fraternal organization. Nathan Tufts, District Attorney of neighboring Middlesex County, also stood accused of taking bribes in exchange for dropping cases. Daniel Coakley, a lawyer and longtime political ally of Curley, allegedly offered the bribes to Pelletier and Tufts.

When Godfrey Lowell Cabot, treasurer of the Watch and Ward Society (a noted Brahmin enclave), publicly accused Pelletier, the Association opened an investigation into the matter. After concluding their inquiry, Bar President Henry Hurlburt turned the evidence over to Attorney General J. Weston Allen who pursued the prosecution of the three men with the assistance of a committee of Bar Association leaders including Robert Dodge, James McCarthy and Andrew

DISTRICT ATTORNEY JOSEPH PELLETIER OF SUFFOLK COUNTY, REMOVED FROM OFFICE FOR BRIBE-TAKING IN THE 1920S, TRIED TO CLAIM THAT THE BOSTON BAR ASSOCIATION WAS PREJUDICED AGAINST ROMAN CATHOLIC ATTORNEYS LIKE HIMSELF. HE RAN FOR MAYOR IN 1921 ON A PLATFORM THAT VILLIFIED THE ASSOCIATION AND ITS ELITIST TENDENCIES.

COURTESY, BOSTON PUBLIC LIBRARY, PRINT DEPARTMENT

Marshall. By 1922, the Supreme Judicial Court removed Pelletier and Tufts from office. Decades later, the Association still pointed to these events as two of its signal accomplishments. Pelletier, however, considered the controversy a case of the "blue bloods" against the "new bloods." Faced with the Attorney General's proceedings against him, Pelletier announced his candidacy for mayor in October 1921. Throughout his campaign, Pelletier played the ethnic card, appealing to ethnic—especially Irish—voters by repeated vilification of the city's Yankee leaders. Many suspected him to be a stalking-horse for Curley's candidacy, put forth to launch ferocious attacks against Boston's best while protecting the former mayor from the political fallout of such tactics. Pelletier's withdrawal and endorsement of Curley just before the election only heightened this suspicion.

Pelletier alleged that a small group of men "from the same caste as the handful who dominate the Bar Association" ran the Good Government Association and other reform groups, using them "to secure control of the political power of this city." Pelletier charged that the conspirators "are always on their toes shrieking their opposition when the people are asserting their right to govern themselves. They fought the initiative and the referendum; they fought the popular election of United States Senators; they fought the direct nomination of candidates for office in the primaries."

Demagogic bombast though it was, Pelletier's rhetoric and the larger political atmosphere of Boston had an impact on the Association. His rhetoric was taken seriously enough that he won an impressive 76,000 votes (out of 176,000) in his failed 1922 bid for reelection to the D.A.'s office. Such support was not lost on the Bar Association; as George Nutter confided in private, the Pelletier situation was "coloring all the Association's acts." The Association recognized the sensitive position it was in when it made a point of recommending an Irishman to replace

COURTESY, BOSTON BAR ASSOCIATION

MILDRED E. BIXBY, ONE OF THE FIRST FEMALE MEMBERS OF THE ASSOCIATION (1926), WAS ALSO ONE OF THE FIRST WOMEN TO SIT ON COMMITTEES, NOTABLY THE MEETINGS COMMITTEE, WHICH SHE SERVED FOR SEVERAL TERMS.

1920 had yielded the same conclusion. But the dramatic changes in the city's bar and the eroding image of the Association called for new approaches. Just as the decision of 1897 to reject permanent quarters symbolized the persisting vision of the Association as the preserve of the bar's best, the long-awaited opening of new quarters in 1927 represented a new understanding of the Association as the voice of a unified bar.

The same pressures that forced the bar to open its membership and decentralize its operations pushed it toward a new home. President Edward W. Hutchins noted in 1916 the need for "a meeting place…to increase social intercourse" to unite the growing and changing bar of Boston. The next president, Samuel J. Elder, continued to urge the acquisition of a building as a way to attract and keep the new members the Association was coming to need so desperately. As yet another Association president, William Caleb Loring, explained, "Without a building of its own, the Bar Association lacks and always will lack cohesion. Without cohesion it cannot hope to do its work with efficiency and to become the power in the community which it ought to be." Loring later offered to give the Association $10,000 toward a new home if enough others would match the offer.

COURTESY, BOSTON PUBLIC LIBRARY, PRINT DEPARTMENT

Frank W. Grinnell, long-time Boston Bar Association member, also served as Secretary of the Judicial Council and of the Massachusetts Bar Association. His legal career spanned decades; here he speaks at a 1962 hearing.

Though all of these men and others had a hand in the reformulation of the Association and the establishment of the headquarters, George R. Nutter led the way. The lifelong Bostonian graduated from Harvard in 1885 and Harvard Law School in 1889. Nutter's life, according to one friend, "was an uninterrupted story of disinterested and influential public service." As president from 1924 to 1927, he spearheaded a number of changes designed to unify and enliven the moribund Association, including the establishment of *The Bar Bulletin* to increase communication and the staging of an annual Bench and Bar Night. He also played a leading role in the revision of membership and Council-election policies. Although his Brahmin pedigree and ties to political reform organizations added to the image of the

Association as an enclave of besieged Yankee reformers, his pursuit of changes in the way the Association operated completed its transformation from an elitist ·organization to a professional interest group.

After a great deal of campaigning by Nutter and others, internal debates and balloting of members, the Association finally officially opened its first permanent headquarters in the new Parker House in June 1927. Although the rooms were rented, Nutter established a building fund to provide money for a future purchase of the Association's own building.

After decades of debate, the decision to move into a new home reflected its awareness of the changes in the profession. "The bar is increasing with leaps and bounds," *The Bar Bulletin* noted, "and with all sorts and conditions of members." The old vision of a socially homogeneous, naturally stratified bar had grown far too incompatible with reality; the Association admitted that "what our members really need is contact with each other; out of which alone comes the public opinion of the bar which must be brought to bear on the many problems of these modern times." As George Nutter put it, "Everyone who is with us in heart must

be welcome to us in presence." No longer would exclusivity be the hallmark of the Association.

The Bar Association of the City of Boston on the eve of the Depression differed greatly from its predecessor of 1900. Its membership was more open, its leadership more decentralized and its assumptions about its role revised. External factors drove those changes. The expansion and diversification of the legal profession in Boston made it virtually impossible for the Association to monitor the ethics and qualifications of the city's bar. Its ventures into the tense public sphere of early twentieth-century Boston proved tarnishing. Deserved or not, the Association quickly earned a label as an organization representing the views and interests of a handful of elitist Yankee lawyers. Stuck with such an image, its opinions could easily be dismissed by legislators and administrators. From an organization of the best of the Boston bar, the Bar Association needed to turn itself into the voice of a unified legal profession in the city of Boston.

AS ATTORNEY GENERAL IN 1929, JOSEPH WARNER CRITICIZED BAR SELF-DISCIPLINE AS "INEFFECTIVE," REFLECTING PROBLEMS WITH MULTIPLE ASSOCIATIONS EXERCISING CONTROL, THE EXPLOSION IN THE NUMBER OF LAWYERS, AND THE LACK OF AUTHORITY ON THE PART OF THE ORGANIZED BAR TO PROSECUTE COMPLAINTS.

The contrast between the new ideal of professional unity and social reality made the future of the Association in 1927 uncertain. The forces of social and political change that had stripped the Association of its earlier conceptions did not appear to be much more compatible with the revised theory of professional identity. It was difficult to see a second-generation-immigrant Suffolk Law graduate sitting down in the Parker House with a Harvard-educated corporate lawyer to discuss the intricacies of a point of law. While the social distance between the two remained wide, the reformed Association of the late 1920s began to make room for both of them. The cacophony of interests competing for attention would continue to expand and, the Association would need to mobilize its diverse constituency into a synchronized chorus.

George Nutter viewed such possibilities with skepticism. "I have grave doubts," he confided to his diary upon stepping down as president, "whether much will be done. I rather think we will sink back into normal and conventional activity. But of course I say nothing." Later he added, "I should like to see what has happened twenty-five years from now." Indeed, a future that included the Depression and the Second World War would offer a new set of challenges both for the bar and for a changed Bar Association of the City of Boston.

COURTESY, BOSTON PUBLIC LIBRARY, PRINT DEPARTMENT

COURTESY, BOSTON PUBLIC LIBRARY, PRINT DEPARTMENT

PROGRESS AND PERSEVERANCE

Leadership and Membership of the Bar, 1927–1957

IF THE ASSOCIAtion under George Nutter experienced invigoration and reorientation, the next thirty years tested how well Nutter's goals would be realized. While the progressive impulse continued, the pressures of depression, world war and cold war impacted strongly on the Association. Still, the stirrings of Nutter's vision remained and the bar achieved a number of important goals in the decades fol-

lowing Nutter's presidency, some of them with the assistance of Nutter himself, who after a term as president of the Massachusetts Bar Association continued to work on behalf of Boston's Bar Association. This activist spirit was passed on to others in the next thirty years: in the vigorous efforts of Damon E. Hall, president from 1937 to 1939, and in the reorienting presidency of Alfred Gardner from 1955 to 1957, during which the modern Boston Bar Association took shape.

In both instances, and in other significant areas, the issues were similar: how the bar association could best serve the practicing attorney and, increasingly, the public. The solution required both organizational and philosophical shifts. Organizationally, the Association became even less centralized and the power formerly vested in the Council was redistributed with the creation of a professional staff and the strengthening of committees. Philosophically, as grievance work began to decline with the emerging importance of the Massachusetts Bar Association, the Boston activists turned their attention outside the bar, to issues of representation and access to legal process which became increasingly important in the 1940s and 1950s. Spurred by due-process abuse during the Army-McCarthy hearings and by emerging Supreme Court doctrine, the Association organized the Boston Bar Foundation in 1957 as its nonprofit umbrella for the various legal aid and study activities that characterize the modern association. And the Association's revamped publication, the *Boston Bar Journal*, first published in 1957, began including more substantive articles and opinion pieces, attempting to

COURTESY, BOSTON BAR ASSOCIATION

HERBERT EHRMANN WAS A YOUNG BAR ASSOCIATION ATTORNEY WHEN HE SERVED AS CO-COUNSEL IN THE APPEAL OF SACCO AND VANZETTI IN 1927. HE BELIEVED THEY WERE UNJUSTLY EXECUTED. THIS BELIEF AS WELL AS HIS ROLE AS COUNSEL DIVIDED THE BOSTON BAR ASSOCIATION, OF WHICH HE WAS A MEMBER.

OPPOSITE: WIDELY BELIEVED TO BE THE VICTIMS OF ANTI-IMMIGRANT, ANTIRADICAL SENTIMENT, NICOLA SACCO, AT RIGHT, AND BARTOLOMEO VANZETTI—BEING LED TO COURT DURING THEIR APPEAL IN APRIL 1927—HAD BEEN SENTENCED TO DEATH FOR PARTICIPATING IN TWO MURDERS THAT OCCURRED DURING A PAYROLL HOLDUP. THEIR APPEAL FOR CLEMENCY FAILED, AND THE TWO WERE ELECTROCUTED IN AUGUST 1927.

give the city's bar a more vital voice than had *The Bar Bulletin.*

"QUIET REVOLUTION": DEPRESSION AND NEW DEAL

George Nutter best summarized the Association's emerging vision at the end of his presidency when he declared, "Our Bar Association is something more than a lunch club with a few disbarments on the side." He continued, "We must be receptive to every new idea" while holding on to "the stability which conservatism gives." In assessing the 1930s, one commentator stated that the decade's challenges and perils "forced the legal world out of that 'rut of respectability'" that Nutter had denounced.

It was the Depression, and the New Deal response to it, that did the most to shape the Association's activities in the 1930s. Characterizing both as "the perceptible if quiet revolution in American life," *The Bar Bulletin* saw the role of the Association as "reforming and...tightening" its own ranks in order to guide this new order well. President Robert Dodge inaugurated the practice of monthly Council meetings (except during the summer) and there was enough business to keep that group at work.

On pressing political causes the Association took a moderate-to-conservative stance. The Sacco-Vanzetti trial and its aftermath was the leading example of this caution. Sacco and Vanzetti, Italian immigrants and self-professed anarchists, were tried and convicted in 1921 for two murders committed during a Braintree holdup. Widely believed to be the victims of anti-Italian, conservative prejudice, the case was appealed in 1926 when two Association members, William G. Thompson and Herbert Ehrmann, attempted to overturn the convictions. The case and the allegation of judicial prejudice split the Boston bar: lawyers liberal and conservative lined up on both sides and worldwide pressure was applied, unsuccessfully, to have the case retried or the governor to grant clemency. Apparently the Council split over the issue, and the division was exacerbated by conflicts between Thompson and George Nutter. Not until after the executions of Sacco and Vanzetti did the Association's leaders state that it would not examine the conduct of the trial judge but would consider general complaints about the judicial system arising from the case. In what was the most debated case of the decade and one of the leading causes of progressives of that generation, the Association remained outside the fray.

Perhaps most symbolic of the Association's essential conservatism was the official attitude toward the great influx of students into law schools during the

1920s. *The Bar Bulletin* carried articles pointing to the huge influx of law students and hence lawyers into the bar in the 1920s, claiming that there would not be enough work for so many attorneys. Certainly the economics of practice were an issue with the mounting Depression; nonetheless, the essential tension may have been the quality of the bar and the ability of the profession to maintain itself as a well-compensated elite. Rather than let market forces prevail, such articles suggested that the Association wished' there were a way to limit the number of lawyers by limiting law school admissions.

Not all of the Association's leanings were conservative, however. In contrast to the effort to derail Louis Brandeis's nomination to the Supreme Court in the

COURTESY, BOSTON PUBLIC LIBRARY, PRINT DEPARTMENT

teens, in 1939, the Council voted its hearty commendation for the nomination of Felix Frankfurter. Frankfurter was a protégé of Brandeis, and like him espoused a liberal approach to judicial reasoning. His status as a professor at Harvard Law School probably made him more palatable to the Council than Brandeis, a practi-

B Y 1927 AUTOMOBILE TRAFFIC ALREADY CHOKED THE STREETS OF BOSTON, BUT MANDATORY AUTO INSURANCE, WHICH BECAME THE LAW THAT YEAR, WOULD CHOKE THE COURTS WITH PERSONAL INJURY AND OTHER LAWSUITS A FEW YEARS LATER.

tioner with whom many members had direct contact. Still, the fact that congratulations were voted at all underscored the leadership's acceptance of both Frankfurter and his ideas, and may indicate a broader acceptance of progressive legal reasoning within the bar at large.

During several signal judicial controversies, the Association, like most of its counterparts, took a decidedly conservative stance. When Governor Curley announced in 1935 his intention to examine for competency all judges over the age of seventy, the bar vehemently demanded "Hands Off!" lifetime judicial tenure. In 1937, the Council took a strong stance against President Franklin D. Roosevelt's court-packing plan, one of the most controversial issues of the decade. Spurred by the Supreme Court overturning of major portions of his New Deal, Roosevelt apparently hoped that by adding additional liberals to the court he could ensure the safety of his political agenda. Attorneys and bar organizations almost universally rejected this idea as unwarranted tampering with the judicial branch; others, however, lauded the idea as a corrective to the out-of-date views of the "nine old men" on the bench. "The shock brought repercussions of a severity still discernible," one chronicler wrote.

COURTESY, BOSTON PUBLIC LIBRARY, PRINT DEPARTMENT

JAMES MICHAEL CURLEY, SMILING FROM HIS CITY HALL DESK IN 1932, WAS A FOUR-TERM MAYOR OF BOSTON, GOVERNOR OF MASSACHUSETTS, AND THE CONSUMMATE IRISH-AMERICAN POLITICIAN. AMONG THE ISSUES OVER WHICH HE AND THE BOSTON BAR ASSOCIATION CLASHED WAS THAT OF LIFETIME TENURE FOR JUDGES.

ACTIVISM IN THE 1930S

Rather than taking stands on leading public-policy or political questions of the day, the Association's reformist tendencies in the 1930s reflected internal house-cleaning activities. Among the accomplishments cited for the decade were growing interest in the integration of bar associations into one, greater activity among bar associations and concern over higher bar admissions standards. One commentator declared that "the profession is becoming alert both to its responsibilities, as well as to its own enlightened self-interest." Nutter's two immediate successors, however, were less activist than he. They did not write articles or editorials for *The Bulletin* as he had done, returning to the kind of stewardship exercised by his predecessors.

Nutter himself returned to the front lines, becoming the chair of the Committee on Legal Education and Admission organized in 1931. Two years later he was instrumental in securing the opinion of the Supreme Judicial Court which held that admission to the bar was a judicial, not a legislative, function. He had a role in framing the new rules on admission to the bar adopted in 1934, which were put into effect over the next several years. These rules answered many of the long-standing objections of members and others that admission to the bar was too easy and attorneys often of poor quality. General education requirements were raised to two years of college study and completion of law school was also required. These requirements made admission to the Massachusetts bar equivalent to that of most industrial states.

This success, coupled with the feelings of dislocation and change produced by the Depression and New Deal, may have sparked another turning point for the Association: a series of informal meetings held in the winter of 1933-34 on how the organization could better serve the bar. Called by respected President Dodge, these talks led to a special committee which recommended an annual reception for new lawyers, lectures sponsored by the Association and a study of the judicial system. To answer emerging interests, a Committee on Criminal Law was added to the list of permanent committees at the annual meeting of 1934. Though Nutter's death in 1937 took a vital leader from the Association, his worthy successor in that role was

Damon E. Hall. In 1937, no doubt at his initiative, the Council created two committees, one "to Ascertain the Views of the Bar of Boston and Vicinity Regarding the Association" and the other to report "on the Enlarging of the Activities of the Association." Despite their windy names, the two committees produced substantive reports. The chief recommendations were for lectures on topics of interest and more cooperation between attorneys on a professional level. The combination became the basis for the Association's sponsorship of continuing legal education.

The first lecture series ever sponsored by the Association, on the progress of a trial, was given by some twenty-nine attorneys and judges in October of 1938 and attracted average audiences of over 500, well in excess of any estimates. Run for profit, the course was highly successful and marked the advent of legal education sponsored by the Association. The series, later published in book form, *From Writ to Rescript*, cap-

COURTESY, BOSTON PUBLIC LIBRARY, PRINT DEPARTMENT

PRESIDENT FRANKLIN D. ROOSEVELT GREETS A FRIENDLY CROWD AT A BOSTON TRAIN STATION IN 1933. THE BOSTON BAR ASSOCIATION'S LEADERS VEHEMENTLY OPPOSED HIS PLAN TO APPOINT MORE JUSTICES TO THE SUPREME COURT IN ORDER TO PROTECT HIS NEW DEAL LEGISLATION.

tured the ABA's annual award for the best legal instruction in the nation for that year. Under Hall, the Association launched a new set of services that would prove critical to its evolving mission.

The idea of continuing legal education remained relatively informal until after World War II, when the Association offered returning lawyers a series of refresher courses on the law. To the surprise of organizers, one-half of the attending attorneys were not returning veterans but lawyers desiring continuing legal education. This response pointed the way toward regular continuing education efforts, in which the Association played an important role. Such legal education in the 1940s often took the form of a lecture series on various topics, such as

THE FACADE OF THE "NEW" SUFFOLK COUNTY COURTHOUSE (1937) REFLECTED THE INCREASINGLY CORPORATE NATURE OF LAW AS WELL AS THE EXPLOSION OF LITIGATION THAT NECESSITATED ITS BUILDING.

medicine and law, and tax. With such lectures, the Association was in the forefront of providing continuing education in the state.

It is not surprising that two of the four founders of the New England Law Institute (NELI) in 1953 were Association members,

Executive Secretary William A. Parks and former Secretary Lowell Nicholson. For a time the impetus for legal education belonged to NELI; the Association's own committee on the subject did not even meet in 1955-56. The need for continuing education, however, would prove so great that soon after the Association became involved it provided more seminars and lectures than ever before. Since the number and type of lectures and programs varied according to demand and to the offerings of other groups, the early programs were the forerunners of the major Massachusetts legal education organizations, including Massachusetts Continuing Legal Education (MCLE), the present leader in programming. (MCLE combined with NELI for a time and in the late 1970s succeeded it as the premier continuing legal education organization until the reemergence of the Association's own programs.)

Legal education was not the only focus of Hall's dynamic term. He also helped to steer a high-profile investigation of the sheriff of Suffolk County, which resulted in the sheriff's removal for malfeasance. In another equally well-publicized case, which an Association member initiated after a chance encounter, an Association investigation spurred the resignation of the Clerk of the Suffolk Superior Court when he was discovered forcing his employees to hand over percentages of their salaries for his campaign fund. Favorable press for the Association emphasized the bar's utility to the public and was viewed with great satisfaction by the leadership, which only a few years earlier might have shunned even favorable reporting.

MODERNIZATION AND BAR ISSUES

The growing complications of industrialized urban life also made their impression on the bar. Boston's population grew from 560,892 in 1900 to 781,188 in 1930; by 1950, the people of Boston numbered over 800,000. This growth brought with it expansion in business, commerce and professional competition among lawyers.

The well-established principle of the prohibition against solicitation of business was reconsidered "in light of modern conditions" in a 1933 *Bulletin* article, which noted how some state bars used the radio to inform the public and reminded members that the Hampden County bar had begun collective advertising. Citing the impersonality of the large city, in which thousands of lawyers competed for business, the article noted that those who solicited benefited from increased business, while deserving members of the public had difficulty in securing competent counsel. One solution, the article noted, was to expect each attorney to devote time to pro bono work in community legal clinics. It concluded that

COURTESY, BOSTON BAR ASSOCIATION

"the usefulness of the bar to the community is drifting downhill…because of adhering to old rules…promulgated to fit conditions of a bygone age."

Trial delays became a major concern of the Association. By 1931, parties to a general suit in Suffolk County waited an average of three years for a jury trial. The Association blamed this delay on the explosion of cases created by mandatory automobile insurance, effective in 1927, which had nearly doubled the caseload from 10,800 entries in 1926 to 18,700 only four years later. Though this problem received some attention in the 1930s, it cropped up again in the 1950s, implying perhaps that a cycle of court congestion and subsequent reform is an enduring aspect of modern litigation.

The impact of modern life told in the way the bar considered its public perception. Press and political scrutiny increased, as when, in 1930, the governor blamed corrupt attorneys for the lax enforcement of standards by bar associations. The Association responded by citing its extensive record in hearing grievances and blamed a lack of cooperation between associations for any shortcomings. In part to answer this and similar criticisms, the Association formed a Committee on Publicity and Public Relations in 1932, a move that a generation earlier would have probably appeared unseemly at best.

FACES OF THE ASSOCIATION: THIS 1941 CARTOON HIGHLIGHTS THE SOCIAL ASPECTS OF THE ORGANIZATION AND ITS REGULATORY AND POLITICAL SIDE AS WELL. SEVERAL FORMER AND FUTURE LEADERS ARE IDENTIFIED, INCLUDING FREDERIC H. CHASE AND WALTER POWERS. ALSO SKETCHED IS AFRICAN-AMERICAN MEMBER WILLIAM H. LEWIS, BY THEN A SENIOR MEMBER OF THE CITY'S BAR AND WELL CONNECTED TO CITY LEADERSHIP.

Perhaps the most telling effect of cultural and social changes on the bar was the constantly voiced concern over the quality and commitment of younger attorneys. While many young attorneys worked as associates with well-established firms, guided by experienced partners, others ventured into solo practices that consisted wholly of motor vehicle torts or conveyancing. In these circumstances, "The Problem of the Young Lawyer," as one article in *The Bar Bulletin* put it, was forming a correct notion of ethical practice. "Having no ingrained knowledge of legal ethics, he cuts corners. Having no experienced older lawyer to guide or stay him he strays…." Several possible solutions to this problem were suggested, including a junior bar and temporary licensing. Clearly the issues posed by a changing legal profession could not be met by such expedients alone.

Membership Trends

Despite its new vigor under Nutter, in 1929 Association membership was 1,731, or about 40 percent of the estimated 4,000 Boston attorneys. The appeal of the Association, judging from new memberships, declined in the years following the Nutter presidency; by 1929-30 the decline had continued for four years. In 1930, the Association announced its ambition to enroll one-half of the practicing bar as members, a goal rapidly eclipsed by the worsening Depression. Numerically the Association continued to represent less than one-half of the city's bar and the organization's reputation remained that of a "Republican-controlled," conservative group, as one Des Moines magazine put it.

This perception was not greatly relieved by the organization's membership profile in the 1930s. While membership from groups such as women, Italians and Jews continued to grow, there was no tidal wave of change. The Association and its leading committees, like the bar, remained dominated by Yankees. Though the first woman was appointed to a committee by President Robert Dodge, who also was president of the Board of Trustees of Wellesley College, female members remained underrepresented on committees for decades, serving largely on minor committees like Meetings; powerful committees, like Grievance, remained exclusively male. Despite the drop in membership, the Committee on Admissions and the Council continued to screen older members of the bar for invitation for admission.

THE BULLETIN BORE EVIDENCE OF NEW INTEREST BY THE RANK AND FILE IN LEGAL EDUCATION, STANDARDS OF ADMISSION AND THE PRACTICE OF LAW GENERALLY.

Although the composition of its membership changed slowly, the membership was not a passive recipient of rulings by Council. *The Bulletin* bore evidence of new interest by the rank and file in legal education, standards of admission and the practice of law generally. Several articles on law school standards appeared in 1938, the year the new admission requirements became fully effective. In the late 1930s, *The Bulletin* also focused on the nuts and bolts of practice, and especially on areas previously untouched, such as criminal law. The bulk of these and similar articles were written by members, some of them unconnected to the leadership or committee system per se. On this foundation, no doubt, the changes of the 1940s and 1950s were erected.

Membership increases and a renewed acknowledgment of diversity, came in the 1940s. The war provided one obvious impetus: with so many members serving in the military and paying reduced dues, the Association needed every full member it could obtain. Dues were dropped in 1941, in part to boost membership, and *The Bulletin* was mailed to all Boston-area nonmembers to drum up new applicants. The result was rising membership throughout the war, and by 1945, membership stood at an all-time high of 2,260. Women, especially, made strides in joining; in 1942, twenty-five became members, increasing by almost 50 percent the Association's total previous female membership of fifty-two. More subtle indications told the tale of the Association's changing patterns of membership, such as a prominently placed *Bulletin* article which commemorated the first Red Mass honoring attorneys and judges ever organized in Boston, celebrated by William Cardinal O'Connor in 1941. In 1948 appeared the first *Bulletin* article written by a woman, longtime member Eleanor March Moody, on the new Boston juvenile delinquent clinic, and in 1948-49, the Association's delegate to the ABA was female member Ines DiPersio.

COURTESY, BOSTON BAR ASSOCIATION

While the Association made some impressive strides in the 1940s, the picture at the leadership level was less sanguine. The Council, which continued to handle much of the substantive decision-making, was the place many Association leaders began their climb. And the Committee on Grievances, drawn from the Council, was a crucial proving ground. Leaders such as Daniel Lyne and Jacob J. Kaplan served on the committee, and by 1930, both Irish-Catholic and Jewish members were regularly elected to Council. Without serving on the Council, members could not be real decision makers, but despite some broadening of representation Council continued to be dominated by native-born Protestant men. The first woman was nominated in

THE MOVE TO 21 SCHOOL STREET, WHERE THE ASSOCIATION HAD ITS HEADQUARTERS ON THE SECOND AND THIRD FLOORS FROM 1941 UNTIL 1952, REPRESENTED AN EXPANSION OF ACTIVITIES, ESPECIALLY SOCIAL ONES.

1941, but hers, as well as subsequent nominations, were unsuccessful until the death of a member led to the elevation of Ines DiPersio in 1952. While the more open nomination process presented more young attorneys for Council positions, in absolute terms leadership representation lagged significantly behind that of the membership at large, a lag most graphically illustrated in the fact that the first Junior Bar Committee in 1936 was all-male at a time when female applicants to the Association were increasing.

As leadership broadened in the Association, its tradition of selecting leading members of the bar continued. Jacob J. Kaplan, the Association's first Jewish president, graduated from Harvard and was editor of the Harvard Law Review before entering a successful practice and being named as a Special District Court Judge from 1928 to 1936. Active in Jewish civic organizations as well as the Boston Symphony and Wellesley College, Kaplan was as professionally respected as his predecessors.

Courtesy, Boston Bar Association

REORGANIZATION AND REORIENTATION: THE 1940S

Despite the leadership lag, the 1940s as a whole were a time of significant change in the running of the Association. A plan to unify the Association's staff work under an executive secretary began under President Damon Hall and culminated in 1940 with the hiring of Lowell S. Nicholson for that post. No longer did key members divide up work among themselves to be done in their own offices. Nicholson, an attorney himself, handled a multitude of tasks, ranging from answering inquiries to editing *The Bar Bulletin.* By far his most important work was as secretary of the Grievance Committee, on which he worked two-fifths of the time. By his own estimate, he handled 90 percent of the complaints himself, without referring them to the committee. As the most visible representative of the organization, he gave a much higher public relations profile to the Association.

DANIEL J. LYNE, BOSTON BAR ASSOCIATION PRESIDENT IN 1941-1942, WAS THE ASSOCIATION'S FIRST IRISH-AMERICAN, ROMAN CATHOLIC PRESIDENT, A HIGHLY SYMBOLIC ELECTION IN AN ORGANIZATION THAT MANY HAD ACCUSED OF ANTI-IRISH, ANTI-CATHOLIC SENTIMENTS DURING ITS HISTORY.

With so much routine work placed in Nicholson's hands, the Association as a whole reallocated its energies in new directions. As Nicholson himself noted in 1945, one area of new expansion was legislative lobbying for and against various bills. Another was more interest in examining discrete issues through special and new standing committees. Finally, the Association contemplated a permanent reorientation away from a primary emphasis on bar regulation and toward public service, though it took more than a decade to achieve.

War service occupied much membership time during the first half of the 1940s. A quarter of the members served in the armed forces and their letters

COURTESY, BOSTON BAR ASSOCIATION

ONE OF THE MAJOR SOCIAL ASPECTS OF THE ASSOCIATION, STARTED IN THE LATE NINETEENTH CENTURY, WAS ITS LUNCHROOM, WHICH ENDURED THE DECADES DESPITE PERIODIC ECONOMIC DIFFICULTIES.   IT IS PICTURED HERE IN 1941.

were frequently published in *The Bulletin*, with a roll of service that was later engraved and installed in the Association's headquarters. Many others participated in the war effort as wardens, volunteers and draft board members. On other fronts, however, the war heightened concerns which had fermented through the 1930s. A 1943 *Bulletin* article bemoaned the loss of business to real estate brokers, accountants and others, and suggested the Association was not doing enough about this issue. While not advocating direct advertising, member Arthur Blakemore suggested that the Association could make known "the remarkable record of the bar in our war effort," root out and expose corruption in the courts, open neighborhood law offices, recommend attorneys competent for motor tort work and inform the public that attorneys could act as bonded fiduciaries, advisers in tax matters and in other capacities. While acknowledging these methods might be "repulsive" to some, the author implied they were necessary, or else "the lawyer of the future must work for a bank or go into the criminal courts." Secretary Nicholson reported that Blakemore's article on "The Duty of the Bar Association to the Ordinary Lawyer" drew more response than any other piece published in the last few years, suggesting the economic anxiety felt by many attorneys.

THE BAR ADJUSTS TO PEACE

War's end found the Association, in concert with other bar associations, organized to assist attorneys discharged from the service in restarting or resuming their practices. Perhaps the single most important contribution made to reintegration of returning lawyers was the series of refresher courses. These courses showed the keen interest of the bar in returning to peacetime normalcy as quickly as possible. Other postwar efforts included assisting with employment, placement services for staff and similar efforts to help attorneys return to or rebuild their practices.

The democratic ideals of World War II made their impression on the Association as the two Association presidents immediately after the war were of immigrant origins. Arthur Santry in 1945, of Irish-Catholic descent, and Judge Jacob Kaplan in 1946, a Jew, were both longtime Council members. Postwar euphoria, as well as intense patriotism, replaced ethnic identification in pursuit of the war effort.

SERVICE AND ACTIVISM

The Modern Bar, 1957–1980

WITH THE NEW DIRECTIONS charted by Alfred Gardner, the Association entered the modern era poised for continued growth. His presidency presaged a period of great change for the Association, and most of his successors embraced the changes he made. Gardner's successors frequently referred to his efforts and those of other activist presidents before him, such as George Nutter and Damon Hall. As the bar struggled with its role in a new world of required representation of criminal defendants, churning political movements and social upheaval, the commitments made by Gardner and other leaders in the late 1950s served as beacons for the modernizing association.

When the tide of social and political change of the 1960s and 1970s swept before it most of the truisms of the past, the Association changed as well, sometimes in response to outside challenges, sometimes leading the way in innovations or reforms. Whereas in the past the judiciary was all but revered by the Association, now individual justices were sometimes strongly criticized. And whereas before many of the more controversial issues of the day had received lit-

tle attention from the Association's leaders, issues such as civil rights, the urban crisis and the war in Vietnam were spotlighted by committees and by the leadership, even in the pages of the *Boston Bar Journal*. By the time the tide turned back toward conservativism, symbolized by the landslide election of President Ronald Reagan in 1980, the Association found itself dissenting from many of the changes affecting law promulgated by the "Reagan revolution."

Finally, as the nature of legal practice changed during this same period, the Association found itself considering both old and new issues directly affecting how law was practiced. The issues of a unified bar, unified procedures, judicial nominating process, changes in discovery and evidentiary rules and other related questions needed to be addressed, and in many instances the Association was directly involved in posing solutions. By the end of this period the practice of law had changed substantively, and

PROPOSED BUILDING FOR THE BOSTON BAR ASSOCIATION LAW CENTER · BOSTON MASS.

COURTESY, BOSTON BAR ASSOCIATION

BEFORE MOVING TO 16 BEACON STREET, THE BAR ASSOCIATION CONTEMPLATED BUILDING ITS OWN HEAD-QUARTERS. IRONICALLY, THE PROPOSED BUILDING BEARS A DEFINITE RESEMBLANCE TO THE ASSOCIATION'S PRESENT HISTORIC HOME.

OPPOSITE: CHILDREN ARRIVING AT THE LEE SCHOOL IN DORCHESTER, A BOSTON NEIGHBORHOOD, IN 1971. THE BOSTON BAR ASSOCIATION WAS DEEPLY INVOLVED IN THE BOSTON SCHOOL DESEGREGATION CASE AND ITS AFTERMATH.

COURTESY, BOSTON PUBLIC LIBRARY, PRINT DEPARTMENT

with it the Association. As litigation continued to grow, as specialties proliferated and as the nature of practice altered, the Association faced the 1980s with much accomplished, but also needing to forge new paths.

MEMBERSHIP AND LEADERSHIP

In many ways, concerns about membership in this period mirrored those of the past: there were not enough members, in the minds of Association leaders, and not enough of them participated in the organization's activities. In 1958, another in a long series of membership drives took place, and the *Journal* was sent to all nonmember Boston lawyers. The Association also undertook a number of radio spots to inform the public about its referral service, both to publicize the service and to improve the image of the bar.

As the committee system grew more elaborate, the Association's leaders worried that members did not participate as fully as they could in the governance of the Association as a whole. Less than one-half of the organization's eligible voters participated in elections, with the exception of 1970 and 1971, when major reform efforts were undertaken by younger bar members and their supporters. Some popular committees enrolled large numbers of attorneys who thereafter did not attend meetings. The dilemma was a familiar one: how to ensure that busy people added one more item to an already crowded schedule.

The modern period saw a sustained interest in the Association's past. President Claude Cross (1957-59), was one of the first to refer frequently to the early history of the Association and to the organized bar of the early nineteenth century from which the Association descended. It was with the presidency of Haskell Cohn, and the approaching Bicentennial of the American Revolution in 1976, that Association leaders linked the 1876 Bar Association of the City of Boston to the colonial and republican associations that existed off and on from the 1760s to the 1830s. This identification has continued to the present.

The path to the Council still lay in serving on a major committee or as a committee chair. In 1956-57, for example, two future presidents chaired key committees: Chester C. Steadman on the Referral Service and Walter I. Badger, Jr., on the *Bar Journal* Committee which oversaw the transition to the new journal format. The vice president now served as chair of the Grievance Committee. Former presidents continued to serve on the Council for life. While women appeared more frequently on committees, they remained outside the leadership circle. A "Women Lawyers' Page" appeared in the *Journal* irregularly from 1959 into the 1960s, but many of the activities reported were not those of the Association itself but of other organizations such as the Massachusetts Association of Women Lawyers. African-American attorneys played a more prominent role in Association activities, with Richard Banks sitting on the ad hoc Planning Committee on Urban Affairs in 1968.

Both in types of practice of its members and in their attitudes, the Association sometimes left a lingering impression of exclusivity. In a memorial to past President James M. Hoy, who died in 1958, the writer noted that his success "should be a stimulating reward to those who made possible" his education at Holy Cross and Harvard Law, cultivating "the brilliant mind of this son of humble parents." As late as 1964, the executive director of the Association introduced a discussion on indigent defense work by noting that "the majority" of members probably had no interest in the issue, as their work embodied "trusts, estates, corporation law and taxation...." In sharp contrast to the leaders of the nineteenth-century bar who were appellate lawyers, President Theodore Chase noted in 1968 that there was little interest among the Association for "the problems of those members who...try cases."

In the city especially, a long-standing social order within the bar had created a power center focused on a handful of large, long-established firms that were physically and ideologically proximate to one another. Often called the "State Street" firms, (though some were situated nearby on Federal, Franklin and other streets), they numbered more than twenty-five partners by 1970, the large majority of whom had received at least one degree from Harvard. There was little integration of minorities or women into the partnership ranks. The mainstay of their practices was corporate law, estates, trust, real estate and counsel work with other major institutions in the state. Pro bono work was relegated to secondary status, usually handed to an associate or other low-ranking member of the firm; there was a social gulf between the large firm attorneys and the smaller firms and scores of solo practitioners whose practices included litigation, criminal defendants or small-

COURTESY, BOSTON PUBLIC LIBRARY, PRINT DEPARTMENT

Governor Foster Furcolo in 1960, the year Boston and Massachusetts Bar Associations tried to hold him to his pledge to consult with both organizations regarding judicial appointments. The Association responded to a rumor that Furcolo was holding a Supreme Judicial Court seat open so that he could occupy it once his term ended in early 1961.

scale probate or real estate matters.

Yet demographics as well as social upheaval were about to change this system permanently. As the first "baby-boomers" began finishing law school and joining the bar, younger attorneys began to increase in numbers. The Association counted 3,513 members in 1970, with an astounding increase by 1980 to 4,918 members. Though older Association leaders continued to worry that the "freshly admitted member of the bar is equipped neither by education nor by know-how to practice unaided," this new generation of attorneys was restless, often eager to see lawyers take on new roles in the social change movements of the 1960s and 1970s. The tensions engendered produced a highly publicized attempt to change the way the Association operated in 1970-71.

In the 1960s, a group of young attorneys known as the "Young Turks" joined together in a concerted effort to reform the Association. Beginning with the Association's ad hoc committee on urban affairs in 1967, this group rapidly coalesced around criticism of the Council for taking overly cautious and moderate stances on pressing issues of the day. Meeting informally at first in the summer of 1968, these attorneys rejected the idea of forming a new association in favor of reform. Trying to work with the new urban affairs section, and rebuffed from playing an immediate role, these attorneys finally bypassed the section chair in mid-1969 to meet directly with new President Haskell Cohn. The result was more representation in the new section, which addressed the proper role of the Association with respect to activism and intervention in urban life.

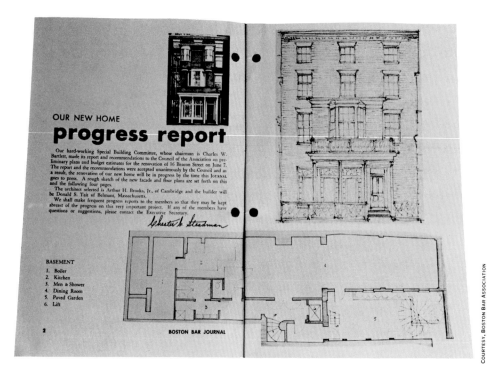

COURTESY, BOSTON BAR ASSOCIATION

THE ACQUISITION AND RENOVATION OF 16 BEACON STREET AS ASSOCIATION HEADQUARTERS WAS A LEADING SIGN OF THE GROWING ACTIVITY AND HIGHER VISIBILITY OF THE ORGANIZATION IN THE LIFE OF THE CITY.

In continuing to apply pressure for reform, Young Turks such as Scott Harshbarger also presented slates of candidates for the first contested council elections in years, those of 1970 and 1971, nominating a much wider spectrum of attorneys than was usually considered for those posts. Several were elected with much higher than usual ballot return rates, and they proceeded to try to speed up the pace of change within the Association. They succeeded in making the Council meetings open to the public and in publishing minutes in the *Journal*, symbolic of their overall attempts to open up the inner workings of the Association. While generational as well as philosophical tensions continued to surround these attempts at reform, the Association was changing, and the outcome was, in the long run, a higher profile by the Association in local and national affairs. Coupled with changes in the State Street world, the reform efforts of the Young Turks continued to bear fruit. As Haskell Cohn put it in the midst of the controversy, "We are conscious of being considered the 'Establishment'...we will continue to try very hard to be 'relevant.'"

THE CIVIL RIGHTS MOVEMENT AND THE ASSOCIATION

As the Civil Rights Movement progressed, Boston attorneys, like many concerned citizens, took stock. In 1963, the Committee on the Bill of Rights—founded to consider anticommunist activity—was asked by the Council "to...cover all the legal phases of the current racial crisis...." President Robert Meserve, later to serve as president of the ABA from 1972 to 1973, defended the new line of Supreme Court decisions, beginning with *Brown v. Board of Education*, as "the only possible answer" to the pressing difficulties of prejudice. In this vein, the Committee on the Bill of Rights, by now having shed its Cold War identity, supported the 1964 Civil Rights Bill and appointed a subcommittee to negotiate with the Boston School Committee and those alleging de facto school segregation. This committee reported a successful outcome, though in fact the issue was merely delayed into the next decade.

In tacit recognition of the links between the Civil Rights Movement and the aspirations of the state's black attorneys, the *Boston Bar Journal* published an article by Charles H. Lewis, president of the Bay State Law Society, in 1967. The society, then the state's professional organization for African-American lawyers, counted sixty African-American lawyers in the entire state, most of whom were solo practitioners, with only one partnership of black attorneys. Lewis further stated that only two firms in the city were integrated. Though there was no direct comment made by bar leaders concerning the article or its facts, the piece occupied the space usually taken by the President's Page. This placement indicates concern on the part of the Association about the place of blacks within the organized bar.

Looking within the profession, Association leaders realized that minorities were often underrepresented among attorneys for lack of financial resources to complete law school. To address this issue, under the presidency of Haskell Cohn, a Special Committee to Assist Minority Students was organized to raise money for scholarships for minority students at the city's six law schools. The committee raised $30,000 in 1970 and $36,000 in 1971, though it seems to have become inactive after 1973. This was the first outreach effort to minority law students supported by the Association.

The Young Turk movement had produced a number of nominations of black attorneys for council seats, and for the first time blacks were serious contenders for the leadership of the association. Under criticism from the Boston NAACP, the Council agreed to include regular representation from the Massachusetts Black Lawyers Association (and, incidentally, the Massachusetts Association of Women Lawyers) on the Joint Committee on Judicial Appointments in 1973. Though it would take nearly twenty years more for the Association to elect its first black president (Rudolph Pierce in 1989), the groundwork for true incorporation of minority attorneys into the Association was laid during this period, and with it commensurate concern with minority issues.

Similarly, women began advancing into leadership posts in unprecedented numbers. Several female attorneys were among the Young Turks and added their voices to the calls for change. In 1974, an ad hoc, all-male committee considered the issue of spouses being named to the same law firms and decided there was no inherent conflict in such a practice. Perhaps in recognition of the underrepresentation of women on important committees, at the same time six women served on the steering committee of the Public Interest Law Office. Women increasingly achieved prominent positions in the Association through the remaining years of the decade, including directing several key projects of the organization, laying the groundwork for the Association's first woman president, Gene D. Dahmen, in 1987.

COURTESY, BOSTON BAR ASSOCIATION

THE ASSOCIATION'S MOVE INTO INCREAS-
INGLY COMMERCE-ORIENTED PROGRAM-
MING IS EPITOMIZED BY ITS CO-SPONSORSHIP
OF INTERNATIONAL WEEK IN THE 1960S.

THE COMMITTEE SYSTEM

The growth of the committee system and later of the section-committee system reflects the growth of the bar as well as the expanding interests of its members. As corporate practice expanded and as more general as well as specialized practitioners were represented in the Association, the committee structure reflected their presence. In 1957, for example, responding to an "alarming increase in family problems," the Association organized a Family Law Committee, whose co-chairs included Boston College Law School Dean Robert Drinan. The Medical-Legal Committee sought to draft a set of guidelines governing expert witnesses, fees and other issues that united lawyers and doctors. These voluntary rules were accepted by the Association, the Massachusetts Bar Association and the Massachusetts Medical Society in the fall of 1968.

Other committees reflected long-standing concerns of the Association. One was the Committee on the Study of Economics and Law, which surveyed the membership in 1959 to help attorneys practice more efficiently, as well as to develop a profile of the income and types of practice of the bar. President Chester Steadman, noting the growth of part-time practitioners, bemoaned this development, apparently in the belief that part-timers took work away from erstwhile full-time attorneys, declaring that a real practice of law "must be...full-time."

In 1968-69, the Association underwent a major reorganization into a section system, modeled after that of the ABA. Areas of great interest, such as taxation, now became sections containing several committees, a structure that has endured to the present. With this change most of the major power to shape Association policy devolved to the committees, completing the transition begun several years earlier. Practitioners could receive substantive information in areas of interest, policy could be made on a variety of fronts and, it was hoped, Association work could be "expedited." Only those members truly interested in a topic were invited to rejoin sections, and objectives were made as clear as possible. Over fifty committees functioned within this system, and a similarly large number of groups, both sections and committees, function to this day.

LEGAL REPRESENTATION

Despite the commitment to legal representation undertaken by the Association, many clients continued to lack adequate counsel. Though usage of the Lawyers' Reference Service ballooned, from 785 clients in 1954 to 3,016 in 1957, the service still operated at a loss. In late 1957, President Claude Cross lamented the "sad fact" that 54 percent of criminal defendants lacked counsel. Like the state's other bar associations, the Association continued to reject the idea of public defenders, preferring that judges appoint attorneys as needed. The organization hoped to attract funds for representation through its Foundation, and Cross pointed out that contributions might "avoid the necessity of you...being appointed" to provide free representation.

This attitude changed rapidly over the next few years as the burden of time on private attorneys escalated. Because of economic concerns, attorneys shifted their support to government-supported legal services as a way to take pressure off the private bar. This concern coincided with the exhaustion of the endowment of the state's Voluntary Defenders in 1959, in response to which President Walter

COURTESY, BOSTON BAR ASSOCIATION

Charles W. Bartlett, Boston Bar Association President (1965-1967), foresaw that unless funding was secured for criminal defense representation, mandated representation would become the responsibility of the private bar. Though the Association continued to handle such defense work on a case-by-case basis, by the mid-1970s plans for legal services were going forward.

I. Badger declared that the Council must take action, noting that more funding was probably not forthcoming. Shortly thereafter the Council voted to support a Massachusetts Defenders Committee, commonly called the "Mass Defenders," appointed by the Supreme Judicial Court. As part of the effort to better inform the public as to their rights regarding representation, the Association, through the Boston Bar Foundation, published a pamphlet, "If You Are Arrested," in 1960. All 25,000 copies were soon distributed, and demand was so great that the Foundation could not afford the desired reprint.

THE ANNUAL RECEPTION FOR NEWLY-ADMITTED MEMBERS OF THE BAR WAS ONE OF THE ASSOCIATION'S MOST POPULAR SOCIAL EVENTS. THIS GROUP WAS AMONG THE ATTENDEES OF THE 1967 RECEPTION.

The growing weight of judicial decisions supported wider and wider rights of representation. After *Gideon v. Wainwright* (1963), all persons accused of serious crimes were entitled to legal counsel and the Massachusetts rules were amended to require counsel in all district court as well as superior court cases. It was clear that the Mass Defenders, a volunteer group, could not handle that volume of litigation. Indeed, the duty of the bar to shoulder the responsibilities of representation was sounded by Executive Director Frederick H. Norton in a *Journal* article entitled "The Gideon Case: A Mandate for the Organized Bar." He suggested the creation of legal clinics, additional funding for the Mass Defenders and perhaps an expansion of the Association's own Lawyers' Reference Service. In 1967, President Charles Bartlett echoed this theme, warning members that if no more government money were given, indigent representation would fall to the private bar, which would receive little or no compensation for such services. Until 1968, however, the Association handled cases on an individual basis, making money available through the Foundation for attorneys handling cases arising from the Roxbury riots and a draft-card-burning case.

COURTESY, BOSTON BAR ASSOCIATION

In 1968, the Association established a Committee on Legal Services to the Indigent to aid the Boston Legal Assistance Project, which coordinated efforts in the private bar to provide legal services. In 1969-70, the committee obtained, through the Bar Foundation, funding for the Boston Lawyers for Housing, a Civil Procedures Project and the Lawyers' Committee for Civil Rights Under the Law. The housing committee, funded from money received from the federal Office of Economic Opportunity (OEO) and the Ford Foundation, was a two-year project to assist in the construction of low-income housing, staffed by three attorneys. Its head was Association member Richard L. Banks. In forming this committee, the Association became the first major city bar association to commit to representing poor clients. Also in 1970, the Association sponsored a noted study, "The Quality of Justice in the Lower Criminal Courts of Metropolitan Boston," which was reviewed in the *New York Times* and distributed throughout the country. The report documented disparate treatment of defendants and a lack of comprehensive rules for administration; its conclusions informed subsequent efforts of the Association to improve legal services.

At the same time, Ford Foundation money became available for neighborhood civil legal services followed by federal money through the OEO. The federal funding of legal services in the 1960s did not solve the problem permanently, however. In 1970, through efforts of the administration of President Richard M. Nixon, the nonpartisan nature of the OEO's Legal Services was threatened. The Council passed a strong resolution in support of continued nonpartisan funding—one of the few associations in the nation to do so. That year, at least, federal efforts to reduce government funding of legal services failed. Assaults on federal funding continued; in 1973, President John G. Brooks warned it would take a "concerted effort" to preserve such services. The Committee on Legal Services of the Association was reactivated during this crisis and the Association lobbied Congress to preserve federally funded legal services. Through the efforts of the Association and other bar groups, the Legal Services Corporation was formed in 1974, a victory for legal services advocates.

COURTESY, BOSTON BAR ASSOCIATION

F. DOUGLAS COCHRANE CHAIRED THE AD HOC COMMITTEE THAT CONSIDERED FORMING A PERMANENT URBAN AFFAIRS SECTION WITHIN THE ASSOCIATION IN 1967-1968. AFTER THE COMMITTEE UNANIMOUSLY RECOMMENDED THE SECTION BE FORMED, COCHRANE WAS NAMED ITS FIRST CHAIR IN 1968.

The Association, in part at the urging of the Young Turks, did not rest with the securing of federal services and funding of a few projects. In 1973, after extensive conferences, the Association agreed to take over and to help fund the Lawyers' Committee for Civil Rights Under the Law, the local branch of a national group of similar committees first formed in 1963 at the request of President John F. Kennedy. With the assistance of the Association's Section on Criminal Law, the committee provided services to a broad spectrum of clients as well as to address public-interest issues such as housing and civil rights. The initial three-year funding run was extended in 1976 for another three years, committing the Association to a long-term legal services project.

In the early 1970s, lawyers throughout the city grew more concerned that legal services were not as available as they could be, especially in the inner-city neighborhoods. Several concerned attorneys called on the Council to do something about this situation. Though there were several providers of legal services, including the Volunteer Lawyers' Project, the Lawyers' Committee for Civil Rights and three firms that made attorneys available for this work, there was no coordination. The Association's Committee on Legal Services to the Indigent reported favorably on an idea to study the situation. In November 1974, the Council voted to host a comprehensive study, the "Action Plan for Legal Services" (APLS), which was conducted by Robert Spangenberg in 1975-76. Including a survey by questionnaire of neighborhoods, service providers and individuals, as well as court observation, the APLS study examined both civil and criminal legal representation and service delivery throughout the city. An Advisory Committee, chaired by Vice President Edward M. Casey, participated in the study. Long-dormant Bar Foundation funds left over from the McCarthy era were used to publish the report.

The study found that due to lack of funding, Greater Boston Legal Services had experienced severe cutbacks in the early 1970s, translating into a lack of services only a few years later. One-third of the poor neighborhoods of Boston had no legal services, with the elderly poor especially hard-hit. There were too few bilingual professionals, too few services for institutional residents, a lack of coordination in existing legal services and inadequate financial planning. Although the study included a strong statement on the obligation of the private bar to provide services, it remained clear that funded legal services would continue to be the mainstay of representation for the indigent. To that end, President John Brooks started the Law Advocacy Resource Center in the early 1970s.

Other initiatives in which the Association participated during this fertile period included the Prisoners Rights Project, launched in 1972 through the Lawyers' Committee under a contract with the Massachusetts Committee on Law Enforcement and Administration of Criminal Justice to provide services to inmates, a few years later becoming an ongoing independent entity; the Urban Legal Laboratory, run by the committee in conjunction with Boston University Law School, founded in 1970 to provide clinical experience to law students; and the Marginally Indigent Defendants' Attorney program, launched in 1974 through the Criminal Law Section and Boston Municipal Court to provide low-cost legal services from a panel of attorneys to poorer clients, an idea that quickly expanded through the city and was copied by other bar associations. In 1976, the Lawyers' Committee filed a federal class action against the Boston Public Works Department, alleging racial discrimination and that the department received an unfair percentage of the proceeds of revenue sharing. Other discrimination suits were filed against municipal police departments for race discrimination and against the Division of Employment Security concerning sex discrimination, among other cases. In 1977, the Legal Services to the Poor Committee, in cooperation with the Boston Municipal Court, set up a cooperating attorney panel for representation of indigent criminal defendants who could not be represented by the Mass Defenders.

COURTESY, BOSTON PUBLIC LIBRARY, PRINT DEPARTMENT

RICHARD L. BANKS WAS A LEADER IN THE BOSTON BRANCH OF THE NATIONAL ASSOCIATION FOR THE ADVANCEMENT OF COLORED PEOPLE (NAACP) IN THE MID-1960S BEFORE RISING TO PROMINENCE IN THE BOSTON BAR ASSOCIATION AS THE ORGANIZATION ADDRESSED URBAN AND CIVIL RIGHTS ISSUES IN THE LATE 1960S.

Clearly, the public-interest aspect of the Association hit an unprecedented high during the 1960s and 1970s.

This pace received recognition in 1976 when the Legal Services Corporation chose the Association as one of nineteen recipients nationwide of special grants to increase the availability of legal services. Prepared by Vice President Edward M. Casey, the grant placed the Association in the forefront of bar associations nationwide that were expanding their legal services work. Basing its application in part on the APLS study, the Association anticipated generating some 3,000 cases through this program and the Volunteer Lawyers' Project, which coordinated volunteer attorneys to handle cases for poor clients. The grant was also used to pay court costs and out-of-pocket expenses of those attorneys involved. The grant allowed the Association to coordinate the services of the Lawyers' Committee for Civil Rights and the Reference Service, both of which advised the project. In the ensuing year, the Volunteer Lawyers Project enrolled 350 attorneys and planned an intensive campaign to enroll even more. The Project also expanded to include legal education in areas such as consumer law

COURTESY, BOSTON BAR ASSOCIATION

EDWARD I. MASTERMAN AT CENTER, CHAIR OF THE DESEGREGATION COMMITTEE OF THE ASSOCIATION, ANNOUNCES PUBLICATION OF *DESEGREGATION: THE BOSTON ORDERS AND THEIR ORIGIN* (1975). HE APPEARS WITH THE BOOK'S CO-AUTHORS, KATHERINE SEAY AND JAMES F. MCHUGH.

and landlord/tenant relations for participating attorneys. By 1979, over 500 Association members participated in the Project, each committed to accepting up to five cases a year. In 1979, the Project, then involving 700 attorneys, received funding for an additional year despite Legal Services cutbacks, with the promise of permanent funding thereafter.

Finally, in 1979, the Association organized the Law Firms Resources Project, overseen by members of the Committee on Legal Services to the Poor, to match Greater Boston Legal Services neighborhood offices with participating private firms in providing support services for cases, ranging from office management to consultation. Further, the Project aimed to involve private sector paralegals in giving pro bono service. This Project was also funded through the Legal Services Corporation, with matching funds given by private firms in the provision of office space and secretarial support. In sponsoring this project, the Association returned, in a sense, to its roots: the ideal that the private bar should, insofar as was possible, undertake to provide pro bono or at-cost representation for needy clients. At the end of 1979, both this Project and the Volunteer Lawyers' Project were taken over for administrative purposes by the Bar Foundation, underscoring the Association's intent to sponsor permanently these projects. In 1980 the ABA recognized all of these legal services projects with one of that year's Harrison Tweed Awards.

THE BAR'S PERMANENT HOME

Perhaps the most important milestone on the Association's social side was the acquisition of 16 Beacon Street, its present home. Following years of renting rooms, the purchase of 16 Beacon in 1962 with the proceeds of the Building Fund begun by George Nutter some thirty-five years before marked the physical embodiment of the Association in a distinguished building, located, appropriately, on Beacon Hill. Ironically, at first the Association had hoped to build new quarters in Government Center, then in the planning stages. Instead, fortune put 16 Beacon on the market, and the special Building Committee appointed to find the Association a permanent home decided to make an offer. With extensive renovations, the building became the Association's new home that fall. The historic building was declared a National Historic Landmark in 1965.

In other respects the social side of the Association reflected changes in the bar generally: as the size of the bar increased, relations between attorneys became more and more formalized. The new bar members' reception continued, but the days of testimonial dinners and smokers were gone. The clublike atmosphere of the Association's offices disappeared; more and more its rooms were used, not for socializing or meals, but for meetings and official business. The lunchroom struggled for business and continued to lose money in the 1960s. Much reduced in scope, it survived this period, but the focus of the Association had moved beyond the clublike practices of an earlier era. Presidents Paul B. Sargent (1971-72) and, later, Raymond H. Young (1981-82) practiced in small firms and sought to reach out to small and solo practitioners. Maintaining and expanding the Association's ties with the courts, President James P. Lynch, Jr., served a partial term before accepting a judicial appointment in 1972.

REGULATING THE BAR

The Association never ceased to perform its function of regulating the bar, and indeed some of its cases received considerable attention. In 1962, for example, the Association fought successfully against the reinstatement of Anthony Centracchio, a former judge who was disbarred for tax fraud and fee splitting in 1954 at the instigation of the Association. In a dispute with Governor Foster

Furcolo in 1960, the Association, together with the Massachusetts Bar Association, attempted to hold the governor to his pledge to consult with the Association regarding judicial appointments. Rumors grew that Furcolo had let a Supreme Judicial Court seat remain unfilled so that, upon his leaving office, he could be appointed to it by his own secretary of state. Some local bar associations, such as Hampden's, Furcolo's home county, defended his right to do so, but the Association denounced this idea. According to both Boston newspapers, the Association's opposition helped dissuade the secretary of state from complying with Furcolo's plan. Thus the Association helped again to preserve what it identified as the integrity of the judiciary.

The Boston Orders and Their Origin

DESEGREGATION

published by the Boston Bar Association

COURTESY, BOSTON BAR ASSOCIATION

DESEGREGATION: THE BOSTON ORDERS AND THEIR ORIGIN ATTEMPTED TO PROVIDE A NON-PARTISAN ACCOUNT OF THE BOSTON COURT-ORDERED DESEGREGATION DECREES FROM A LEGAL STANDPOINT. THE BOOK WAS WIDELY READ BY THE PUBLIC, AND THE ASSOCIATION MADE MEMBERS AVAILABLE TO DISCUSS THE LEGAL ASPECTS OF DESEGREGATION AT COMMUNITY MEETINGS.

Another prominent case, which underwent careful scrutiny by Association members, involved the readmission of Alger Hiss to the Massachusetts bar. Hiss, a Harvard-educated international law expert in the 1950s, had been convicted of passing atomic secrets to the Soviets during the McCarthy era and had been disbarred as a result. Urged to reapply in Massachusetts by former President Claude B. Cross, Hiss appeared before the Council in 1974. After an "extended discussion," the Council voted that his readmission to the bar would "not be detrimental" to the law. Upon his readmission the following year Hiss joined the Association and its international law section. With his readmission, perhaps, came a symbolic end to the wounds created by the anticommunist movement of the 1950s.

The question of who judged judges was thrown into high relief by the Troy case in the late 1960s. Judge Jerome Troy was Chief of Dorchester District Court and was accused of unfair and inconsis-

objections centered on the unequal amount of power to be granted to nonurban areas of the state under the unification proposal set forth. The Association did, however, recognize the need for a more unified approach to bar discipline, and so backed in its counter-proposal a board of examiners for the bar to handle complaints. After several years of debate and the appointment of a special master to review rival proposals, the Supreme Judicial Court set up a Board of Bar Overseers in 1973 to examine complaints against attorneys, modeled on the Association's proposal. Included in this proposal was a provision for a clients' security fund to reimburse clients whose attorneys misappropriated their funds. With the Court's action, the issue of a state bar was seemingly resolved; Massachusetts would continue to exist with multiple bar associations, though with a unified approach to discipline.

Finally, the changes to practice inaugurated with the United States Supreme Court's decision in *Bates v. State Board of Arizona* in 1977, lifting the ethical bar against advertising by attorneys, was the object of intense scrutiny in 1977-78. The Association appointed a special committee to study the decision and make recommendations to bring the Massachusetts Code of Professional Responsibility into compliance. Though cautioning against the possible expense and rate-cutting that advertising might produce, President Joseph Bartlett suggested that the freedom to advertise might be used to give smaller practitioners access to higher visibility by placing group announcements through the Lawyers' Reference Service, which in turn could screen clients for participating attorneys. Thus the decades-long concern with the position of the practitioner continued to occupy the attentions and efforts of the leadership.

The rapid changes in practice were often linked to the role of continuing legal education, specifically the ongoing role of the Association in providing that education itself and through MCLE. In the late 1960s, the leaders of various associations and of MCLE and NELI arranged coordination of programs so that overlap was eliminated. The Association, for example, had long given a federal tax seminar every year, and that became one of its education areas. In 1969, the Association turned over the responsibility for the profit and loss of its programs to

Action Plan
for Legal Services

Part 2: Report on Criminal Defense Services to the Poor in Massachusetts

Sponsored by the BOSTON BAR ASSOCIATION
By: William J. Rose and Robert L. Spangenberg

COURTESY, BOSTON BAR ASSOCIATION

THE ASSOCIATION'S ACTION PLAN FOR LEGAL SERVICES STUDY FOUND SIGNIFICANT LACKS IN LEGAL SERVICES FOR THE POOR IN BOSTON. THESE FINDINGS HELPED SPUR BOTH ASSOCIATION AND PRIVATE BAR EFFORTS TO IMPROVE SERVICES IN THE NEXT DECADES.

SECTIONS AND COMMITTEES OF THE
BOSTON BAR ASSOCIATION

ADMINISTRATION OF JUSTICE SECTION
Gender & Justice Committee

BUSINESS LAW SECTION
Antitrust Committee
Banking Law Committee
Bankruptcy Law Committee
Commercial Lending Committee
Computer Law Committee
Corporate Counsel Committee
Corporate Law Committee
Energy Law Committee (jointly sponsored with the
    Environmental Law Section)
Insurance Law Committee
Intellectual Property Committee
Lawyers for the Arts Committee
Legal Opinions Committee
Securities Law Committee
Sports and Entertainment Committee
Tax-Exempt Organizations Committee

CRIMINAL LAW SECTION

DELIVERY OF LEGAL SERVICES SECTION
HIV/AIDS Committee
Lawyers Public Interest Responsibility Committee

ENVIRONMENTAL LAW SECTION
Clean Air Committee
Energy Law Committee (jointly sponsored with the
    Business Law Section)
Environmental Litigation Committee
Hazardous Waste Committee
International Environmental Committee (jointly spon-
    sored with the International Law Section)
Legislation Committee
Solid Waste Committee
Water Quality & Treatment Committee
Wetlands & Waterways Committee

FAMILY LAW SECTION
Family Law Committee

HEALTH LAW SECTION

INTERNATIONAL LAW SECTION
Immigration Law Committee
International Business Transactions Committee
International Dispute Resolutions (jointly sponsored
    with the Litigation Section)
International Environmental Law Committee (jointly
    sponsored with the Environmental Law Section)
International Financial Transactions Committee
International Tax Committee (jointly sponsored with
    the Tax Section)

Public International Law Committee

LABOR AND EMPLOYMENT LAW SECTION
EEO/Discrimination Law Committee
Employee Benefits/ERISA Committee
Individual Employee Rights Committee
Labor Law Committee
OSHA/Workers' Compensation Committee

**LAW OFFICE MANAGEMENT, ECONOMICS AND
    PROFESSIONALISM SECTION**
Professional Ethics Committee
Solo and Small Firm Practices

LITIGATION SECTION
Alternative Dispute Resolution Committee
Appellate Committee
Business Litigation Committee
Federal Practice and Civil Procedure Committee
Intellectual Property Litigation Committee
International Dispute Resolutions Committee (jointly
    sponsored with the International Law Section)
Massachusetts Practice Committee
Professional Liability Committee
Tort Committee

PROBATE LAW SECTION
Estate Planning Committee (jointly sponsored with the
    Tax Section)
Probate Law Committee

REAL ESTATE SECTION
Commercial Real Estate Financing & Development
    Committee
Condominium & Cooperative Committee
Equity Financing Committee
Leasing Committee
Residential Conveyancing Committee
Title and Title Insurance Committee
Zoning & Land Use Committee

SENIOR LAWYERS SECTION

TAX SECTION
ERISA Committee
Estate Planning Committee (jointly sponsored with the
    Probate Law Section)
Federal Tax and Business Transactions Committee
International Tax Committee
State and Municipal Tax Committee
Tax-Exempt Organizations Committee (jointly spon-
    sored with the Business Law Section)
Tax Practice & Programs Committee

YOUNG LAWYERS SECTION

MCLE, while retaining a role in sponsoring the content of the programs. The Association continued to offer a handful of programs that it had pioneered and built over the years, such as the Labor Law Institute run in conjunction with Boston University Law School. In 1979-80, MCLE incorporated and the Association gave it support to ensure it would survive.

The era from 1957 to 1980 saw the emergence of the Association as an activist organization, embracing a range of concerns far beyond its traditional scope. Spurred by social crisis, internal and external criticism and the changing opinions and ideals of its members, the Association adopted an extended commitment to legal services, took a vigorous role in the modern form of bar regulation and discipline and helped usher in a new era of unified legal education. From these changes there was no turning back, and with few exceptions the membership welcomed this new set of priorities. As an advocate and provider of legal services, however, the Association would find itself in conflict with the new conservatism of the 1980s. This conflict would put the Association in a new, not unwelcomed position: in opposition to the status quo, which increasingly denounced legal services, or at least government funding of them, as inimical to current ideas of law and order. The sometimes painful, but in the end, valuable conflicts and disputes of the late 1960s and early 1970s had put the Association on a new path and by 1980, the extent of change was such that there was no turning back; indeed, the Association pointed with pride to the battles fought during the 1980s to protect its vision of the law.

COURTESY, HARVARD LAW SCHOOL ART COLLECTION

ALGER HISS, EDUCATED AT HARVARD LAW, CLERK TO JUSTICE OLIVER WENDELL HOLMES, RISING STAR IN INTERNATIONAL RELATIONS, WAS CONVICTED OF BEING A SOVIET SPY IN 1950, IN A CASE THAT FIRST BROUGHT HIS ACCUSER, RICHARD NIXON, TO PROMINENCE. IN 1975, WITH THE ACQUIESCENCE OF THE BOSTON BAR ASSOCIATION, HISS WAS READMITTED TO THE MASSACHUSETTS BAR.

EPILOGUE

Ongoing Activities of the Bar

THE PROMISE OF THE ASSOCIATION AS an active and vibrant professional and public service organization has been most fully realized since 1980. Its leadership has reorganized and revitalized the Boston Bar Foundation and has undertaken several initiatives within the city and the state to promote justice and reaffirm the Association's commitment to community affairs. The Bar Association vigorously increased the membership and active participation of women and racial minorities. It elected its first female and first black presidents (Gene D. Dahmen and Rudolph F. Pierce) in the late 1980s, backed the ultimately successful movement for mandatory IOLTA (interest on lawyers' trust accounts) funding of legal services and played a major role in lobbying for increased funding for the state court system.

This vigorous activity was often the result of external forces and circumstances. Despite concerted efforts in the 1980s by the federal government to dismantle the Legal Services Corporation (LSC), Association Presidents John J. Curtin and Raymond Young led effective lobbying efforts to preserve it. Curtin later served as president of the ABA (1990-1991). While funding sources for the LSC were reduced, individual states and bar associations scrambled to make up the lost money from state and private sources; the Bar Association became a leader, once again, in that effort to fund legal services for the poor.

By the 1980s, the public service activities of the Association included the Lawyers' Committee for Civil Rights, the Boston Municipal Court Project, the Lawyers' Reference Service, the Suffolk Bar Advocates Program, the Law Firms Resources Project, the Volunteer Lawyers' Project, the Law Advocacy Resource Center and the Volunteer Lawyers for the Arts. The Volunteer Lawyers' Project alone received over 5,000 requests for services and produced an estimated 11.5 million dollars in legal services for the indigent in the 1979-80 fiscal year. Adding to the existing demands on Boston's private bar was not easy. Mindful of its deep and historic commitment to equal justice under the law, Association President John Perkins reminded the members in 1983 of the legacy of John Adams and Josiah Quincy's defense of British soldiers charged with murder in the Boston Massacre in 1770.

CRAIG BAILEY

THE U.S. DISTRICT COURT, DISTRICT OF MASSACHUSETTS, IS LOCATED IN THE STATELY POST OFFICE AND COURTHOUSE BUILDING IN DOWNTOWN BOSTON.

OPPOSITE: ESTABLISHED IN 1803, THE SOCIAL LAW LIBRARY IN BOSTON SERVES AS THE MAIN RESEARCH LIBRARY FOR THE COURTS AND PRACTICING BAR.

KELLER AND PEET ASSOCIATES

Nearly 200 years later, the tradition of equal justice under the law is the continuing commitment of the Association.

In late 1981, the Association began to solicit large firms to permit junior associates to serve training rotations within legal services to help provide needed legal representation. Several firms had signed on to this project by early 1982. Private funding sources also materialized, including what was probably the Association's first challenge grant, a $100,000 matching grant from the Permanent Charities Fund to endow legal services funding. Bar Association members and leaders were involved in the effort to enact the Massachusetts Legal Assistance Corporation (MLAC) in 1982. Finally, to take advantage of tax changes, the Association consolidated all of the various legal services projects under the Boston Bar Foundation in 1983-84, and the Foundation's Advisory Council, which included past Association presidents as well as others, was reorganized to undertake fund-raising for both Association and Foundation activities.

COURTESY, BOSTON BAR ASSOCIATION

RUDOLPH PIERCE WAS THE FIRST AFRICAN-AMERICAN ELECTED PRESIDENT OF THE BOSTON BAR ASSOCIATION, IN 1989–1990. HIS PRESENCE AT THE HEAD OF THE ORGANIZATION WAS AN INDICATOR OF HOW FAR AFRICAN-AMERICANS HAD COME IN BAR MEMBERSHIP FROM THE CIVIL WAR ERA, WHEN ONLY TWO AFRICAN-AMERICANS PRACTICED LAW IN BOSTON.

Among the initiatives launched in the late 1980s was petitioning the state to allow IOLTA participation, particularly by the efforts of Katherine McHugh, a successful endeavor that has since funded numerous public service law projects. Keeping up with current pro bono areas also led to new projects within the Foundation, including the Lawyers Clearinghouse on Affordable Housing and Homelessness, cosponsored with the Massachusetts Bar Association, which, by 1990, had provided over one million dollars in services.

The battle over the future of the LSC, probably the most divisive debate within the national legal community during the 1980s, fueled, in part, the decision of the Council to formulate a strategic plan for the Association in 1985-86. President Richard Renehan authorized the development of the first major strategic plan for the Association. David Rideout, president-elect, chaired the strategic planning committee, an innovative endeavor which broadened the leadership and identified the major issues of the future. Facing continued fiscal strains in trying to meet indigent defense needs as well as a growing roster of public-policy issues, the Association focused on furthering delivery of legal services to the poor and section and committee work on substantive legal issues. In 1988, the Council heightened its involvement in civic affairs.

By the mid-1980s, the federal and most state governments had taken aim on what was proclaimed to be an epidemic of drug use and drug-related crime and violence throughout the nation. President Edward F. Hines appointed a special task force in 1988 to consider the issue and announced in its 1989 preliminary report that a comprehensive program was needed to combat the epidemic, including education and job training for inner-city residents and expanded drug-treatment programs. The report did not endorse what were popular political measures, such as mandatory sentencing of drug dealers, viewing them as unlikely to achieve an overall reduction in drug use and drug-related crime.

Another epidemic, that of AIDS, is receiving attention from the Association. The disease, which came to affect tens of thousands of Massachusetts residents, had long been overlooked by the legal profession. In 1991, the Bar Association set up its first pro bono program to assist people with AIDS who needed legal representation, while the Boston Bar Foundation began to offer grants to public service organizations providing such services.

The Association, long an advocate of raising judges' salaries and improving courtroom conditions, pursued the improved administration of justice under President William Looney (1985-86). The Association also began a Court Support Program in 1988-89 to match large firms with district courts in Suffolk County. Over the entire decade, the Association backed legislation to repair, upgrade and improve the courts and their services as well as compensate their staffs adequately. Though such bills faced uphill battles in fiscally conservative times, the Association continued its efforts in the name of expediting justice.

THE MODERN BAR ASSOCIATION HAS A MISSION FAR BROADER THAN EVEN THE MOST VISIONARY BOSTON ATTORNEY OF 1760 OR 1876 COULD HAVE FORESEEN.

The 1980s also witnessed the rapidly changing demographics of the bar, which nearly evened the sex ratio of newly admitted attorneys by 1992. The presence of growing numbers of women attorneys led to new interest in family issues such as child care for working parents and the ways in which firms hired and promoted associates. By the 1990s a quarter of the Association's membership was female, as was nearly half of the Council. The Association participated in the Gender Bias Study, commissioned by the Supreme Judicial Court and published in 1989, devoting its entire July/August 1989 *Boston Bar Journal* issue to the report and the questions it raised for women judges, attorneys and clients alike. In 1989, the Association commissioned a task force on family employee benefits to address a major issue of the decade.

Concurrently, historic strides were made by minorities in entering law throughout the United States and in Boston. Determined to address the issue of membership, the Association formed a Committee on Minorities in the Profession in 1987-88 to promote outreach to the city's minority attorneys; the effort was extended in 1990 by a joint conference of the Bar Association and various minority bar associations on the problems affecting minority attorneys. As President Rudolph Pierce observed in 1989, in the less than twenty years he had been a member of the bar, the Association had come a long way from the "stodgy, conservative white male club" he remembered.

The variety and sheer number of practitioners and practices made maintaining contacts with individual attorneys an increasing challenge. That, and a demand for utilitarian service from the Association, led to a renewal of continuing legal education efforts. The Bar Association supported the incorporation of Massachusetts Continuing Legal Education, Inc. (MCLE) in 1979-80, but also found it necessary to begin its own slate of programs, both alone and as a cosponsor, during the 1980s, including training for lawyers involved in various pro bono efforts. Long a pioneer in continuing legal education, particularly under the guidance of Haskell Cohn, a national leader in the field, the Association today offers diverse programs with lecturers from large and small firms as well as related fields.

The economic growth of the 1980s and the concurrent explosion of people entering law led to spectacular growth of firms, especially those with nationwide, even international, operations. In a variety of areas, the Association harnessed the energy, efficiency and economic support of the large firms in Boston to continue to define and expand a collective vision of the public interest.

Yet this growth was followed in some cases by equally spectacular collapse. Among the casualties were some of Boston's oldest, best-known law firms. As the economy contracted further, familiar concerns reemerged about whether the profession could support the rising number of lawyers entering it and the increasing level of litigation, which many believed made the United States the most lawyer-heavy and litigious nation in the world. Whether the profession would need to make major changes was a question often asked but still deferred as the 1990s began.

The new decade found many of the issues long addressed by the Association still unresolved. Representation of indigent and marginally indigent clients was still of concern, even though more resources than ever before were being committed to that effort by private practitioners and firms as a result of funding shortfalls within the state's own services. The so-called "war on drugs," waged through mandatory sentences, was not working to prevent recidivism or to stem the flow of drugs into neighborhoods, but neither were the alternatives proposed by the Association's task force finding widespread accep-

COURTESY, BOSTON BAR ASSOCIATION

SANDRA L. LYNCH, BOSTON BAR ASSOCIATION PRESIDENT IN 1992–1993, WAS A LONGTIME ASSOCIATION MEMBER WHO HAD SERVED ON SEVERAL COMMITTEES, INCLUDING THE LONG-RANGE PLANNING COMMITTEE IN THE LATE 1970S, GIVING HER A UNIQUE PERSPECTIVE ON THE FUTURE OF THE ASSOCIATION.

tance. Acknowledging that full representation of the Bar Association continued to be a concern, the first three presidents of the 1990s—John P. Driscoll, Jr., Margaret H. Marshall and Sandra Lynch—all reiterated the Association's need to reach out to women and minorities even more.

What is most striking about these very real efforts to effect change was that they reflected the training and vision of a new generation of attorneys, the same generation that had lobbied for change in the early 1970s. Coming of age in the mid-1960s and later, these attorneys saw the law as an instrument of change as well as being a public trust. Seen in that light, the astonishing array of issues that the Association has addressed has the same kind of community cohesion the original Suffolk County Bar Association had over two hundred years ago: the goal of affecting the practice of law to make it better. The thirty-three counsellors and barristers of colonial Boston sought to enhance the public interest by regulating admissions and, occasionally, their practice; the nearly 8,000 members of the 1990s Boston Bar Association do so across a remarkably broad range of professional and social issues.

COURTESY, BOSTON BAR ASSOCIATION

Legal services continues to occupy center stage in Association concerns. Here Volunteer Lawyers Project Director Meg Connolly is pictured with Delivery of Legal Services Co-chair Leslie Klein and Dwayne Deskins, U.S. Attorney's Office, in 1989.

The modern Bar Association, then, has a mission far broader than that envisioned by its founders, born out of a membership far wider than even the most visionary Boston attorney of 1760 or 1876 could have foreseen. In spite of its conservative roots, the Boston Bar Association has become a leading voice of moderation, even liberality, in defending the public interest during a time of conservative political efforts to reduce support for legal services and fiscal restraint that hampers efforts to fund the court system. The Association is in the stewardship of leaders who are aware that token representation, whether of clients or within its own membership, does not serve the purpose of true integration.

The generation of lawyers that has come of age since the 1960s has a wholly different face than any generation preceding it. The Boston Bar Association has remade itself to reflect this newly heterogeneous bar, destined to become even more varied in the next century, rather than to return to the homogeneity of the last century. As its leaders repeatedly remind constituents, there is more to be done; but if the pace of change since 1970 is any indication, the next twenty years will again find the Association transformed.

PARTNERS IN EXCELLENCE

THE HISTORY OF THE Boston Bar Association is thoroughly enmeshed in the fabric of Boston's own history. With roots reaching back into the eighteenth century, the Bar has long been a witness to and participant in the events that have shaped each successive era. This tradition continues today as members of the Bar actively engage in almost every sector of professional life in the city.

From the courtroom to the boardroom, Boston's attorneys may be found at work litigating before the bench or negotiating across a table. These professionals are preparing contracts, providing counsel, and defending the rights of businesses and individuals.

Practicing in the fields of corporate, real estate, probate, banking, copyright, and tax law, to name just a few, the area's attorneys provide expertise in every area. They are able to do so in today's fast-paced, ever-changing environment by continually anticipating their clients' needs. If changes in legislation are to affect the workplace, the marketplace, or the place one calls home, Boston's attorneys are among the first to know—and react accordingly. By utilizing this information to further their clients' interests, these highly trained men and women demonstrate their dedication to meeting the needs of the people they serve.

This dedication extends to the community at large as well. Members of the Bar generously donate their time and efforts to work on the numerous public-service committees established by the Association. The Volunteer Lawyers Project, to name just one, provides millions of dollars in legal services for the indigent every year.

B OSTON'S HISTORIC WATERFRONT UN-
DERWENT SIGNIFICANT REBUILDING
AND DEVELOPMENT IN THE MID-1980S. MANY
BOSTON LAW FIRMS, INCLUDING SOME OF THE
OLDEST, MOVED INTO THIS NEWLY INVIGORAT-
ED AREA OF THE CITY DURING THE SAME ERA.

This blend of high-minded professionalism and civic responsibility has been a hallmark of the Bar and its membership down through the years. It is exemplified today by the law firms whose profiles follow, beginning on page 140. Each gives testament to the best the Bar has to offer.

As impressive as the history and present-day exploits of the Boston Bar are, this history could not have been written, indeed could not have been made, if it weren't for the efforts of the devoted professionals who work in the ancillary sectors of the Boston legal community. Their essential goods and services, skillfully supplied, provide the final pieces in the mosaic that is the Boston legal community. The stories of these Friends of the Bar begin on page 188.

COURTESY, BOSTON BAR ASSOCIATION

BOSTON BAR ASSOCIATION

SINCE ITS FOUNDING IN THE 1760S BY A group of Boston attorneys led by future U.S. President John Adams, the Boston Bar Association (BBA) has served the professional needs of its members and has endeavored to seek positive change in the greater Boston area. The nation's oldest bar association, the BBA has also been one of its most innovative, in areas ranging from legal aid to volunteer mentoring of the city's youth. The association has long taken a leadership role in bar regulation, professional development of attorneys, and legislative initiatives across a range of legal issues.

From the historic first meetings of the Suffolk bar in taverns, to the nineteenth-century "smokers," to the committee meetings of the present, the Boston Bar Association has accommodated the changing pace and emphasis of bar organization. The association has long provided its members with a wide range of personal and professional services from its headquarters at 16 Beacon Street, a renovated brick townhouse on the National Registry of Historic Places. With its expansion into 18 Beacon Street in 1993, the organization can now offer even more, keeping pace with its mission of service to the profession.

PHILOSOPHY

In serving member needs, the Boston Bar Association has endeavored to keep pace with changing times and with the spectacular growth of the legal profession, both in overall numbers and in specialization. Pledged to meet the needs of all of its 8,000 members, the association has within

the last decade revitalized its continuing legal education programs, added new member benefits, and encouraged the establishment of new committees to better reflect practice specialties.

While member service is an important part of the association's mission, the organization is just as dedicated to its ongoing commitment to the city of Boston. The association brings its members' expertise and interest into play within greater Boston, and within the commonwealth, on a wide variety of issues ranging from public education to combating drug abuse.

SECTIONS AND COMMITTEES

The lifeblood of the Boston Bar Association is its section and committee structure. The existence of active sections and committees in a wide variety of legal specializations allows individual members to hone their skills and provides leadership to the bar as a whole. Section meetings and educational efforts provide one of the most vital services to members while at the same time enhancing legal practice and professionalism as a whole.

SUBSTANTIVE PROGRAMS

The association has organized and currently supports a number of substantive programs intended to address important issues. The Committee on Minorities in the Profession, for example, not only works to promote racial diversity within the association, but within the legal profession as a whole, providing training to firms on strategies to increase minority hiring. In the late 1980s the Task Force on Parenting

neys at Berlin, Clarey handle a wide range of matters directly. In the event that outside specialists are brought in on a particular aspect of a project, the firm ensures that such assistance is closely overseen and coordinated with the other client services being provided. The firm additionally offers its clients full litigation support for those disputes carried into court.

By combining its legal expertise with its appreciation of the close interrelation of clients' business and personal needs, Berlin, Clarey, Axten & Levee has built a flourishing practice that it looks forward to furthering in the years to come.

(FROM LEFT) NEWTON H. LEVEE, LAWRENCE P. FRAZER, GERALD A. BERLIN, PHILLIPS AXTEN, AND RICHARD D. CLAREY.

GUILD, MONRAD & OATES

GUILD, MONRAD & OATES, INC., (GMO), a firm specializing in the management of investments for individuals and families, was founded in 1983 by four Harvard-educated businessmen: Henry R. Guild, Jr., Ernest E. Monrad, William A. Oates, Jr., and Robert B. Minturn, Jr. GMO is located on the top floor of 50 Congress Street, near the new Post Office Square park and garage. Guild, Monrad, and Minturn are members of the Massachusetts Bar.

The cornerstone of GMO's expertise is investment management for clients by its principals in their capacities as personal trustees. Total assets under management by the principals in various capacities exceed $500 million.

As a registered investment advisor, the firm also furnishes investment advice and management on an agency basis to individuals and other fiduciaries, such as partners in law firms and managers of charitable endowment funds. Additional services GMO provides include tax-return preparation and tax and estate planning. Individual principals of GMO serve as executors of clients' estates.

GMO focuses its management skills on a limited number of portfolios with a long-term investment outlook. The firm's business has grown rapidly as clients increasingly seek a haven where investment management, tax matters, estate planning, and administration of estates can be handled for them by seasoned professionals in a single office.

(LEFT TO RIGHT) HENRY R. GUILD, JR., ROBERT B. MINTURN, JR., BRUCE H. MONRAD, WILLIAM A. OATES, JR., GORDON C. BARRETT, AND ERNST E. MONRAD.

DUNN AND ROGERS

THE BEACON HILL LAW FIRM OF DUNN and Rogers was founded in 1932 by Charles J. Dunn, Sr. He was joined in the practice of law by his brother, John F. Dunn, in 1936. For many years the firm flourished in a small office in Barrister Hall, just outside Boston's old and bustling Scollay Square. The firm quickly built a reputation as one of the premiere medical malpractice defense firms in the City of Boston, with the Dunn brothers representing physicians, nurses and hospitals.

CHARLES J. DUNN, JR., JOHN F. DUNN, AND WILSON D. ROGERS, JR. (LEFT TO RIGHT).

After Charles J. Dunn, Sr., passed away in 1983, the mantle of leadership of the firm was assumed by Charles J. Dunn, Jr., and Wilson D. Rogers, Jr. John F. Dunn continues to practice with the firm in addition to serving as chairman of the Board of Bar Examiners, a position to which he was appointed by the Supreme Judicial Court of the Commonwealth of Massachusetts.

While the defense of medical malpractice cases remains a major facet of the firm's practice, over the last 20 years a substantial corporate practice has also evolved. The firm represents a number of hospitals and other non-profit or charitable organizations. In 1984 His Eminence, Bernard Cardinal Law, Archbishop of Boston, appointed Wilson D. Rogers, Jr., as general counsel to the Roman Catholic Archdiocese of Boston. In this capacity,

Rogers serves as chief legal advisor to the Cardinal Archbishop of Boston, overseeing all of the legal services rendered within the Archdiocese of Boston.

From 1973 through 1982 Charles J. Dunn, Jr., helped influence the makeup of the Massachusetts bench by serving on Governor King's Judicial Nominating Committee.

From the small office in Barrister Hall with two lawyers, the firm has grown over the course of the years to 10 attorneys in elegantly appointed offices at 20 Beacon Street.

Both Charles J. Dunn, Jr., and Wilson D. Rogers, Jr., emphasize the strong influence on their professional lives that was exerted by Charles J. Dunn, Sr. Dunn describes his father as a hard-working, dedicated attorney who worked actively at the firm up until his death at the age of 82. Rogers sums up: "I think everyone is influenced in his professional life by one person. In my case I am fortunate to have had that person be Charles J. Dunn, Sr. He was an extraordinarily gifted attorney who combined an exceptional work ethic with the highest ethical and professional ideals. I would hope, as we follow today in his footsteps, that he is pleased with what we have done with the firm."

BENJAMIN & BENSON

WHEN DOMESTIC BLISS TURNS SOUR, HUS-bands and wives in search of a civilized way out of their marriage often wind up at the Cambridge law offices of Benjamin & Benson, a firm with a reputation for bringing dignity to what by nature are nasty negotiations.

Benjamin & Benson is a boutique firm with two partners—Roberta Benjamin and Jon Benson—who concentrate solely on matrimonial law, or, as Benjamin puts it, "dispute resolution at its most basic." The firm handles divorce cases, custody suits, paternity work, and a limited amount of wills and trusts.

Founded on the belief that marital woes need not engender full-scale war, Benjamin & Benson takes a personal approach to guiding families through their problems. That means the firm learns as much as possible about the backgrounds of its clients, ranging from the kids' schools to details of child or alcohol abuse in the families of origin.

"We don't operate as a factory. We try to create a family atmosphere," Benjamin explains. "At our best I think what we can do is enable people to structure their lives during a time of great stress to the benefit of the entire family and to hopefully minimize the adversarial nature of the process.

"We try very hard to be there for clients and they truly appreciate it. We have established a lot of good will and some lasting friendships," adds Benson.

The first session of the superior court once operated in the refurbished, red-brick building where Benjamin &

Benson located upon its start-up, in January 1985. Benjamin and Benson met three years earlier, while representing opposing interests in a divorce proceeding. As they continued their respective career paths—she at a large law firm, he as a solo practitioner—they found themselves increasingly consulting each other on matters of family law and thus decided to formalize their informal affiliation.

ATTORNEY PHYLLIS KOLMAN, ATTORNEY ROBERTA BENJAMIN (SEATED), AND JOHN PETERSON.

Although business is brisk, Benjamin and Benson have no plans to expand beyond the one associate they now employ. The firm is in a comfortable economic position that affords its attorneys for the most part the luxury of picking and choosing clients. Benjamin says, "We only represent people who we would go out to dinner with."

Benjamin, however, frequently serves as a court-appointed attorney for children in contested custody cases, a role she says often exposes her to psychologically disordered parents. "The reason cases don't settle at that level is you're not simply dealing with nice people in situational stress; you're frequently working with people in stress who bring with them historical baggage from their own families of origin and background that they carry into the situation," explains Benjamin. "It's a tough job."

MARY BETH SWEENY, ATTORNEY JON BENSON, AND COLLEEN CANNON (LEFT TO RIGHT).

LOONEY & GROSSMAN

LOONEY & GROSSMAN WAS ORGANIZED IN 1965 by four former assistant U.S. attorneys, who together charted an early course for the firm in the areas of white-collar

(BACK ROW, LEFT TO RIGHT) ROBERT C. BARBER, WILLIAM F. LOONEY, JR., AND STEWART F. GROSSMAN. (FRONT ROW, LEFT TO RIGHT) BRADLEY W. SNYDER, RICHARD J. GRAHN, BERTRAM E. SNYDER, AND RICHARD J. LEVIN.

criminal defense, commercial litigation, workouts for distressed businesses, and bankruptcy law. The firm has undergone several changes to its administrative guard since its inception, along the way broadening its range of service-oriented expertise to also include a full range of corporate and real estate services.

With seven partners and 11 associ-

ates, Looney & Grossman today remains a mid-sized law firm, with a downtown Boston office at 101 Arch Street, guided by its original vision of a flexible, quality-driven firm that could handle complex cases and solve legal problems of the utmost urgency.

William F. Looney, Jr., one of the firm's founding partners, sums up the foundation upon which Looney & Grossman is built: "All during the life of the firm we have operated what you could almost describe as an emergency room for individuals and businesses involved with legal disasters. We tend to represent clients who have serious troubles."

Bankruptcy reorganization, business restructuring, and workouts constitute a significant aspect of the firm's work. Here again the firm's lawyers most often come to the defense of clients with severe business problems.

Legal problems that the firm also deals with on behalf of individuals include such charges as tax fraud and securities fraud brought by federal and state authorities. The firm represents people in Federal Deposit Insurance Corporation investigations and grand jury investigations that call into question government contracts. The firm also defends officers and executives from banks and other financial institutions who are implicated in wrongdoings within larger cases.

Mindful of the high costs associated with bankruptcy and litigation, however, Looney & Grossman strives to resolve disputes out of the courtroom. The firm emphasizes reorganization rather than liquidation, while orchestrating fair settlements for clients that range from mom-and-pop enterprises to multimillion-dollar companies. When bankruptcy reorganization matters require court action, the firm is able to assemble a team of experts to respond quickly and skillfully. Many of the firm's attorneys are trained and experienced in the bankruptcy reorganization area of law.

Looney & Grossman lawyers have also served as trustees in dozens of bankruptcy cases, in which capacity they have operated a diverse range of companies. This experience has gained them firsthand insights into the daily challenges that decision makers face. These insights translate into valuable advice that strengthens the legal counsel clients seek.

In the last half-dozen years, the firm has doubled in size, and with that growth the focus of the firm has expanded to meet the corporate, real estate and general business and litigation needs of a wide range of businesses and financial institutions, as well as individuals. Specific areas of expertise in which the firm excels include complex secured lending on behalf of banks and other financial institutions, intellectual property and software licensing, and transportation situations including admi-

ralty, aviation, and trucking matters. Although the firm has remained relatively small, it has gained the necessary expertise to offer a wide range of services. Nevertheless, the firm prides itself on continuing to offer personal attention and flexibility while attending to complicated business and litigation matters.

Looney & Grossman lawyers are called upon to represent entrepreneurs engaged in new business opportunities. The firm's attorneys recognize and act decisively upon the critical role that timing can play when entrepreneurs are embarking on new ventures. They do so by working swiftly and closely with clients to identify needs, goals, and, when appropriate, alternative courses of action. Because risktaking tends to beget problems, the firm both helps entrepreneurs strategize around potential damage and structure transactions so that they can meet their short-term and long-term objectives.

Looney & Grossman continues to assign top priority to progressive cases and activities. Some of the firm's most notable milestones reflect the liberal spirit that guided its early beginnings, including helping to found the National Lawyers Committee for Civil Rights in Boston, and representing the Boston Latin School Association, on a pro bono basis, for 14 years in the Boston school desegregation case.

In keeping with this heritage, Looney & Grossman encourages its attorneys to become involved in community and social service activities. The firm's lawyers are active participants in various bar associations, charitable entities, and law school alumni organizations.

SCHNEIDER, REILLY, ZABIN & COSTELLO

STANDING BEHIND HIS DESK AT THREE Center Plaza, Albert P. Zabin recalls the words of Babe Ruth, who, when told the Boston Red Sox would offer him a contract, reportedly replied, "You mean they're really going to pay me to play baseball?" "That's how I feel sometimes," says Zabin about the small law firm for which he has worked since 1962.

In startling contrast to many Boston firms that employ an excess of 100 lawyers, Schneider, Reilly, Zabin & Costello consists of seven trial lawyers. "We try very hard to stay small," says Zabin, managing partner. "We turn a lot of prospective business away to stay small." Instead the firm sees itself as an elite group that will litigate only claims that are "substantial," involving $250,000 or more, or those that interest the lawyers personally.

While its early reputation was built on success in winning record awards in personal injury cases, the firm has gradually moved into business litigation, trying complex cases involving patents, products liability, and trade secrets that often relate to advanced technology and intricate legal issues.

With a general trial practice in all courts, Schneider, Reilly, Zabin & Costello also litigates cases in the areas of

JOSEPH SCHNEIDER, FOUNDER OF SCHNEIDER, REILLY, ZABIN & COSTELLO.

admiralty, personal injury, antitrust, railroad, medical malpractice, and aviation law. The firm handles commercial zoning, toxic tort, insurance, intellectual property, and appeals cases.

Partners Joseph Schneider and Joseph E. Reilly started the firm in the 1930s. It was Schneider who determined much of the firm's tenor and direction—not only because of his irrepressible character, but because the firm lost Reilly in 1956, when he was killed in an accident on the Southeast Expressway. A Russian immigrant, Schneider was a varsity boxer at Boston Latin School. Before he entered Harvard College, he attended Boston University Law School for two years. He read for the bar, in the days when one could, and eventually became the first Jewish president of the Massachusetts Bar Association. His wife, Esther L. Schneider, practiced law alongside him, an unusual practice even today. He was also one of the founders of the organization that became the Association of Trial Lawyers of America.

Apart from his leadership roles within the profession, Schneider was considered an expert personal injury lawyer. He won what was, at the time, the largest award in Massachusetts in a personal injury case—$300,000—against Peretti Brothers Construction Company for a client who suffered brain damage on the job. Schneider continued to practice law in the firm he founded until his death in 1985.

It was Schneider's reputation as a skillful and exacting trial lawyer that brought Zabin to the firm upon graduating from Harvard University Law School. With the addition of two young lawyers, Zabin and, in 1973, Robert V. Costello, the firm entered a new period. "Schneider always appreciated aggressive boxer types and lawyers with broad interests," says Zabin of the new team.

Between 1965 and 1988 Schneider, Reilly, Zabin & Costello tried more than 10 landmark cases, most of them in the field of tort law. Some of the precedents the cases established include: foreseeable misuse of a product is not a defense to a negligence claim against the supplier of the product; comparative negligence is not a defense to a breech warranty; and a college owes a duty to its resident students to use reasonable care in protecting them from assaults by third persons.

In 1971 Zabin won the largest products liability case in Massachusetts up to that time. In this case a scuba diving vest manufactured in Massachusetts by New England Divers had failed and caused the death of an Alabama dentist. The case was further complicated because the accident occurred in Okinawa, Japan. Although the case was tried in the state, Massachusetts law required that Japanese law govern the outcome. Zabin had to educate himself on points of Japanese law and enlist the assistance of several Japanese as expert witnesses and translators.

In the spring of 1974 the whole firm was brought to the test. The federal court in Boston decided to catch up on its civil docket and clear a pool of backlogged cases. Over a period of eight weeks the firm won 10 of its 11 cases. This frantic time was a turning point for the firm, re-establishing its reputation in the world of litigation.

Some of the firm's notable cases in commercial litigation have involved damages resulting from stolen trade secrets. In 1983 the firm represented an inventor who charged American Permac and its German parent corporation dry cleaners with breach of contract in failing to exploit an automated garment retrieval system Willis had devised. The case drew on testimony from a robotics expert at the Massachusetts Institute of Technology. At the trial's conclusion, Willis received $2.85 million verdict.

Zabin, a frequent contributor and former associate editor of the Massachusetts Law Quarterly, is the author of "The New Wrongful Death Act in Massachusetts," an article often cited by the Massachusetts Appeals Court and the Massachusetts Supreme Judicial Court. More recently Zabin co-authored a textbook, entitled *The Disability Handbook,* with Dr. Alan Balsam. Costello was a founder of the Massachusetts Bar Association's Computer College and is a frequent lecturer for continuing legal education programs for the Massachusetts Bar Association and the Massachusetts Academy of Trial Lawyers.

Most of the cases the firm litigates touch on disciplines besides law, says Zabin. He and his colleagues relish the constant learning process these cases demand, often turning to the firm's technical library, which is nearly as large as its law library. Over the years, lawyers at Schneider, Reilly, Zabin & Costello have been trained as engineers, pilots, and nurses.

ALBERT P. ZABIN AND ROBERT V. COSTELLO.

TEDESCHI, GRASSO AND MORTENSEN

TEDESCHI, GRASSO AND MORTENSEN IS located in the business and financial center of Boston with a satellite office in Providence, Rhode Island. The firm was organized in 1987 by several attorneys with experience in finance, commercial and business transactions, and litigation. Tedeschi, Grasso and Mortensen provides business and litigation services to clients ranging from individuals to high-tech development corporations, manufacturers, and publicly held companies.

The firm's business and corporate division provides active representation requiring a wide range of skills and knowledge, including financial and technical knowledge related to clients' businesses

The firm also offers a full range of services in real estate transactions, including site acquisition and development, financing, lending, and sales. Tedeschi, Grasso and Mortensen represents clients in biotech, trade secrets, and intellectual property areas and provides services to companies engaged in manufacturing, software and intellectual property licensing, and regulated transportation.

The firm is active in the areas of mergers and acquisitions and the sale of businesses, as well as the representation, restructuring, and liquidation of corporate subsidiaries.

Tedeschi, Grasso and Mortensen has experience and expertise in state and federal securities laws, advising clients concerning securities regulation and the purchase and sale of securities.

The firm also has substantial experi-ence in director and officer liability insurance and fidelity bond matters.

Partners of the firm have been engaged by public companies in connection with investigations and enforcement actions relating to the activities of the issuer or its management by the United States Securities and Exchange Commission and the securities administrators of various jurisdictions. The attorneys in these areas work closely with the attorneys in the litigation department.

The business and corporate group also provides commercial law services including venture capital financing and commercial loan documentation, secured transactions, and debt restructuring and workouts.

The firm's trial and appellate litigation practice regularly handles a variety of complex matters for businesses and corporations ranging widely in size.

The litigation attorneys regularly appear in the state and federal trial and appeals courts. Litigation matters include business torts and contracts, securities law, antitrust law, commercial cases, foreclosure and bankruptcy matters, trade secrets and intellectual property cases, environmental matters, insurance coverage litigation, and personal injury litigation. The firm also handles arbitrations and actions before government agencies and self-regulating organizations.

Tedeschi, Grasso and Mortensen is structured to provide effective and economic service that is consistent with current business realities.

WEINGARTEN, SCHURGIN, GAGNEBIN & HAYES

WEINGARTEN, SCHURGIN, GAGNEBIN & Hayes traces its roots back to World War II, when founding partner Joseph Weingarten served as senior patent counsel for the U.S. Navy. Weingarten practiced in the vanguard of super-advanced electronics work conducted by the Navy in the famous MIT Building 20 and Radiation Laboratory, and soon became known in almost every front office of the Massachusettes high-technology industry for both his congeniality and his ability as an intellectual property attorney. In 1956 he founded the Law Offices of Joseph Weingarten, which expanded and matured along with the high-tech field itself.

Today the firm consists of 15 lawyers who practice all types of intellectual property law, including litigation; negotiation and drafting of technology licensing agreements; patent, trademark, and copyright prosecution; and, of course, client counseling. A common thread that ties these subspecialties together is personalized attention to client needs, which reflects the highly individual demands that drive intellectual property law.

Intellectual property is perhaps one of the most fluid areas of the law, due to influences of divergent practices of intellectual property protection observed by foreign countries and forces working to adjust and harmonize those systems in an ever-shrinking world. Against this backdrop Weingarten, Schurgin, Gagnebin & Hayes handles an increasing volume of international work. The firm maintains professional relationships with dozens of attorneys and patent agents in technically sophisticated countries around the world, enhancing its representation of clients in the U.S. and abroad.

Over the years attorneys at Weingarten, Schurgin, Gagnebin & Hayes have fostered interest and change in intellectual property law in various ways. The firm's attorneys teach patent and copyright law as professors at local law schools and conduct seminars in various aspects of intellectual property law. Their keen interest in technology also draws them into "basement workshop tinkering," the type of hands-on engineering exercises that went part and parcel with their early training in technical subjects. Several members of the firm command advanced technical degrees and experience in the hi-tech industry.

MANAGING PARTNERS CONSULT IN THE WEINGARTEN CONFERENCE ROOM OVERLOOKING THE NEW PARK AT POST OFFICE SQUARE.

The attorneys' extensive technical training gives rise to one of the pleasures of their practice: addressing specialized technical issues with clients, assessing their needs quickly and efficiently, and responding in kind. That not only benefits clients, but also keeps Weingarten, Schurgin, Gagnebin & Hayes out at the frontier of innovation, where the ideas protected today promote the technology of tomorrow.

VACOVEC, MAYOTTE & SINGER

VACOVEC, MAYOTTE & SINGER IS A LAW firm distinguished for its concentration in tax law. Attorneys at Vacovec, Mayotte & Singer bring a blend of specific legal experience, creative planning, and extensive

PARTNERS OF THE FIRM (CLOCK-WISE FROM BELOW CENTER) KEN VACOVEC AND ANN TRUETT, MAUREEN MAYOTTE, JEFFERY BROWN AND ANN TRUETT, AND PAULA SINGER.

knowledge to a diverse range of client matters.

Founded in 1978 as a tax firm, Vacovec, Mayotte & Singer is built on a foundation of quality service. The addition of attorneys with extensive experience in banking, high-tech, accounting, consulting, and insurance, as well as in private practice, has expanded the firm's capabilities to meet the legal and tax needs of business and individual clients.

The focus of the firm is sophisticated

tax planning and related legal services for high-net-worth individuals, estates, and closely held companies. The firm advises these clients on both domestic and international tax matters where the firm has developed extensive experience. The firm's approach is to develop tax-effective strategies to meet business and individual clients' needs and to advise clients of the resulting tax compliance requirements. The firm represents clients before federal and state tax authorities, guiding clients through audits and other complex proceedings before these government agencies. Because of the firm's unique experience, the firm frequently acts as special tax and legal counsel to other professional advisors on behalf of their clients.

From its inception, the firm has provided international tax planning for executives relocating internationally. As a result of this work, the firm has expanded services to include foreign and domestic income and estate tax planning for individuals as well as international tax planning for businesses operating in our global economy. Firm attorneys have years of practical experience dealing with both tax and totalization treaties of the United States. To service the needs of its international clientele, the firm has established a network of corresponding tax and legal counsel in more than 50 locations worldwide.

The attorneys at Vacovec, Mayotte & Singer stand ready to provide quality domestic and international tax and legal services to individuals, businesses, and to the legal and financial communities.

O'CONNELL AND O'CONNELL

O'CONNELL AND O'CONNELL WAS founded by Joseph F. O'Connell, Sr., in 1897 and remains under the family aegis today. Joseph Sr., educated at Boston College and Harvard Law School, opened the firm in the Fields Corner section of Dorchester. The firm moved to downtown Boston at 53 State Street, in 1906 and remained there until the early 1930s, when it moved briefly to 11 Beacon Street before going to its present address, 31 Milk Street, in 1935.

Joseph O'Connell, Sr., was elected to the 60th and 61st U.S. Congress. His brothers, James E. and Daniel T. (Don), joined the practice in 1908, making the firm J.F., J.E., and D.T. O'Connell. The firm's practice has always been general in nature and included representation of the Irish government; Don O'Connell pressed the cause of Irish independence in Washington following World War I. He served on the Massachusetts Superior Court from 1928 to 1958.

Two of O'Connell's eight sons, Joseph Jr. and John T.L. (Lenahan), joined the firm in 1938. With the death of Joseph Sr. in 1942 and seven sons away in the service, six as officers, the firm's practice was managed by their aunt, attorney Margaret Lenahan. After the war, Joseph Jr. and Lenahan returned to the firm and were joined by a younger brother, Fredrick P., several years later. Joseph Jr. died in 1966 and Fredrick in 1991.

Joseph Sr. also served as manager of Boston's George Robert White Fund from 1938 to his death and was the first member of the Boston Bar Association to be elected as a delegate to the American Bar Association's House of Delegates. A member of many bar associations, as were all his sons, Joseph Sr. was also the Massachusetts chairman of the Commission on Uniform State Laws at his death. Joseph Jr. practiced before the state and federal courts, the U.S. Supreme Court, and the Philippines Supreme Court. He was also a member of the A.B.A.'s House of Delegates and the Commission on Uniform State Laws. Lenahan has served as trustee of the Boston Public Library, the Boston Museum of Fine Arts, and the Social Law Library. He carries on the family's tradition of public service while maintaining its legal practice nearly a century after the founding of O'Connell and O'Connell.

ABOVE: ATTORNEY JOSEPH F. O'CONNELL PHOTOGRAPHED AT HIS LAW OFFICE DESK IN BOSTON, MASSACHUSETTS, ON THE AFTERNOON OF HIS DEATH, DECEMBER 10, 1942.

LEFT: SEATED (LEFT TO RIGHT) ARE, BOB PRICE AND CHARLES H. BURTON, WASHINGTON, D.C., SECRETARY AND JUNIOR BAR SECRETARY, A.B.A.; FRANK GRINNELL, DELEGATE, MASSACHUSETTS BAR ASSOCIATION TO A.B.A.; AND LENAHAN O'CONNELL. STANDING (LEFT TO RIGHT), ARE JOSEPH F. O'CONNELL, JR.; STANLEY BROWN, NEW HAMPSHIRE; JIM POWERS, (WNAC); BOB SIEGEL; ALBERT WEST; AND LAWRENCE CORCORAN. ALL WERE PRESENT FOR THE 1948 PRESENTATION BY FRANK GRINNELL, STANLEY BROWN, AND CHARLIE BURTON OF THE A.B.A. AWARD TO THE MODERATORS OF THE BAR ASSOCIATION FORUM AND WNAC.

WOLF, GREENFIELD & SACKS, P.C.

WOLF, GREENFIELD & SACKS, P.C., founded 65 years ago, ranks among the largest intellectual property firms in New England, and among the most experienced firms in the country. Headquartered in Boston's Federal Reserve Building, and having a vast network of associates in more than 100 countries, the firm commands a far-reaching reputation as an accomplished legal guardian of innovative ideas.

THE FIRM'S ATTORNEYS BRING THEIR KNOWLEDGE AND EXPERI-ENCE TO BEAR ON ALL ASPECTS OF CLIENT MATTERS.

Within the specialized realm of intellectual property law, the firm provides a sweeping range of services, such as patent, trademark, and copyright protection; trade secret protection; licensing; international technology transactions; entertainment industry transactions; joint ventures; franchise and distribution agreements; confidentiality agreements; software licenses; and related litigation. Clients that enlist Wolf, Greenfield & Sacks include multinational, national, and local corporations; major academic institutions; distinguished hospital and independent research institutions; small entrepreneurial companies and engineering firms; individual inventors; and creative talents.

FOUNDING PARTNERS (LEFT TO RIGHT) GEORGE GREENFIELD, DAVID WOLF, AND STANLEY SACKS.

Ezekiel Wolf founded the firm in 1927. His son, David Wolf, carried on the practice, along with partner George Greenfield, after Ezekiel died in 1958. Stanley Sacks, the third named partner, joined the practice in 1961. The firm expanded slowly but surely up until 1987, when 19 attorneys practiced with the firm. Since then the firm has doubled in size to nearly 40 attorneys and a staff of 130 that includes technical specialists, paralegals, and support workers.

Wolf, Greenfield & Sacks' patent

practice provides timely preparation and prosecution of patent applications in the United States and in virtually every other country that offers intellectual property protection. Their attorneys, some of whom are former patent examiners, bring their technical knowledge and experience to bear on all phases of patent prosecution, including appeals and interference proceedings, reissues, and reexaminations. The firm has orchestrated the protection of major technological breakthroughs, providing the economic leverage for its clients to obtain the full value of their intellectual property and the economic incentive to turn important ideas into products that benefit the general public. In 1991 alone, its attorneys filed more than 800 patent applications in the U.S. and 20 other countries.

The trademark division of Wolf, Greenfield & Sacks files scores of applications to register words, logos, phrases, and designs as trademarks and service marks. The firm assists clients in all aspects of protection—ranging from design to domestic and foreign searches of existing marks to acquisition and licensing. As part of the extensive process, the firm polices the marketplace for possible copycats, and litigates when infringement does occur.

For example, Tootsie Roll Industries is renowned for Tootsie Roll candy bars in the orange and brown wrapper with twisted ends. Attorneys at Wolf, Greenfield & Sacks advised the candy company that consumers recognize the product as much for the wrapper as for the Tootsie Roll trademark, and secured a series of trademark registrations that protected the distinctive wrapper. When another company began selling a different product with a different name, but in a wrapper indistinguishable from Tootsie Roll's, the wrapper trademark helped bring a speedy end to the infringement.

In the area of intellectual property litigation, Wolf, Greenfield & Sacks is one of the most active firms in the Northeast, representing clients throughout the country and, through correspondent firms abroad, in courts worldwide. The firm's attorneys have argued before the U.S. Supreme Court and regularly appear before federal trial and appellate courts, the International Trade Commission, state courts, and such administrative boards as the Trademark Trial and Appeal Board.

Wolf, Greenfield & Sacks is also highly regarded for its entertainment and copyright practice, which has blossomed in recent years. Members of the music, art, theater, audiovisual, and literary communities turn to the firm for the skills and sensibilities that diverse creative endeavors demand. In practical terms, that means the firm's entertainment specialists represent musicians in multiple capacities—as attorneys, agents, or advisors—in securing recording contracts, negotiating agreements, and protecting material. In the motion picture area the firm structures financial arrangements for features and negotiates option, distribution, and story rights agreements. Its attorneys were the first to bring and litigate a case under the pioneering Massachusetts "moral rights" law protecting the integrity of art works.

A vigorous copyright practice encompasses such major areas as fabric design, packaging, and toys and games. The firm specializes in advising the holders of the rights—often small businesses or individuals—in all matters relating to the business of their art. Conversely, the firm represents clients—typically large corporations—in obtaining rights for the use of copyrighted materials and advising them in issues related to the reuse of material, such as music, text, photographs, and graphics, owned by others.

WOLF, GREENFIELD & SACKS REPRESENTS CLIENTS THROUGHOUT THE COUNTRY.

WOLF, GREENFIELD & SACKS PROVIDES A SWEEPING RANGE OF SERVICES.

WIDETT, GLAZIER & McCARTHY

WIDETT, GLAZIER & McCARTHY IS A goal-oriented firm dedicated primarily to providing basic business services. Partners and associates pay special attention to smaller businesses, guiding them through entrepreneurial rigors ranging from start-ups to bankruptcies. "We're closer to small business clients because we are a small business ourselves," notes partner Marijo McCarthy.

A CORRIDOR CONFERENCE WITH PARTNERS, MARIJO McCARTHY AND IRWIN GLAZIER.

Senior partner Irving Widett founded the firm in 1979 after branching off from a practice he had established with his brother 40 years earlier. The success of Widett's first firm was double-edged. It expanded into such a large operation that Widett missed the intimacy and efficiency of a small firm environment and, at age 65, decided to retire. Upon urging from many of his clients, he instead opted to continue practicing a more personalized style of law by launching Widett, Glazier & McCarthy with, initially, a former associate, Irwin Glazier.

In its fledgling days the firm concentrated on bankruptcy law, bolstered by Widett's deeply entrenched bankruptcy practice. The firm has since broadened its representation to provide critical legal services to companies engaged in many walks of business, among them manufacturing, professional services, and the restaurant industry.

TEAMWORK AT ITS BEST—WIDETT, GLAZIER & McCARTHY WORK TOGETHER FOR THEIR CLIENTS.

In addition to providing bankruptcy advice, the firm specializes in corporate legal services ranging from incorporation and litigation to collection matters to drafting and reviewing contracts, leases, and employment agreements, and assisting banks with new loans, loan workouts, foreclosures, and civil litigation.

Widett, Glazier & McCarthy is located at 90 Canal Street, in the historic Bullfinch Triangle. The firm's partners and associates assign a lion's share of research and paperwork to law clerks. This team structure allows the firm to provide more cost-effective services for clients as well as groom a pool of team-oriented talent from which it often hires associates.

Mindful of the risks associated with getting a business off the ground, attorneys act not only as counselors, but also as objective business consultants. When new clients confront seemingly simple questions outside the legal framework, the firm encourages them to seek fee-free advice about the possible repercussions of their decisions. That's a role that invites what McCarthy and her partner, Glazier, describe as "hand-holding," which in turn builds confidence and nurtures relationships.

"You can't tell businesspeople what to do, but you can make them stop and think about what they want to do. That's how we see our role as small-business lawyers," says Glazier.

MELICK & PORTER

MELICK & PORTER IS A FIRM FOCUSED on litigation, trying cases in state and federal courts. Founding partners Richard Melick and Thomas Porter opened the practice in January 1983 with a twofold vision: to give clients the highest level of professional service possible, and to create a community of people who respected and enjoyed working with one another.

Dick Melick has been a trial lawyer for 36 years. He has also served for 30 years as Needham Town Moderator and as an officer of numerous professional and charitable organizations.

Tom Porter has been a trial lawyer for 18 years. He chairs the editorial board of the *Journal of Law and Religion*. He also serves on the board of Union Theological Seminary, in addition to working for other professional and charitable organizations.

In keeping with the founding partners' philosophy, Melick & Porter supports the pro bono activities of its attorneys and encourages involvement in charitable and community organizations. Twice each month all attorneys gather to reflect on changes in the law and in the practice, including trial techniques.

The firm's clients include universities, hospitals, doctors, manufacturers, large and small businesses, insurance companies, and individuals. Practice areas include all types of malpractice, product liability, toxic and hazardous waste, general liability, and all other tort litigation areas, as well as many commercial litigation areas.

The firm has grown from five attorneys and two secretaries to its present staff of 23 lawyers, of whom 14 are partners; 12 secretaries; 17 paralegals; and six support staff. The practice maintains a sophisticated computer system for data organization and document retrieval that is critical to the smooth progress of complex litigation.

In 1990 the firm moved from its original quarters on Arlington Street in the Back Bay to One Joy Street, Beacon Hill. The firm is only the third owner of this historic building, constructed by the Shaw family in the 1830s. In 1890 the building became the headquarters for the Episcopal Diocese of Massachusetts. A number of illustrious Bostonians have resided and worked there, including Robert Gould Shaw, commander of the 54th Colored Regiment during the Civil War, and the charismatic Bishop Phillip Brooks. Melick & Porter

MELICK & PORTER OFFICES, ONE JOY STREET, BEACON HILL.

have restored and refurbished the building to provide a warm, enjoyable atmosphere for both clients and firm members.

During the past decade Melick & Porter has established a tradition of excellence that it will strive to enhance into the next decade and the next century, heeding the initial goals of excellence in service and a collegial atmosphere.

STANDING (LEFT TO RIGHT), JEFFREY MELICK, GEORGE WAKEMAN, RICHARD SHEA AND STEPHEN SUTTON. SEATED, THOMAS PORTER AND RICHARD MELICK.

O'Connor, Broude & Aronson

FOR A DECADE, O'CONNOR, BROUDE & Aronson has provided expert services to its clientele of emerging businesses and entrepreneurs. Founded in 1983, the firm has grown to 10 attorneys, plus five paralegals and a full support staff, in keeping with the growing needs of long-time and new clients. This steady growth will continue in order to provide the ongoing services the firm's clients expect, and to keep pace with the business and investment climate of the New England region.

Its partners, Dennis O'Connor, Paul D. Broude, and Neil H. Aronson, made the initial decision to locate O'Connor, Broude & Aronson in the heart of Boston's technology region on Route 128, "America's Technology Highway." The firm's attorneys believe they can better serve their clients, many of whom are in the area, from the firm's offices at the Bay Colony Corporate Center at Route 128 and Winter Street in Waltham than from a downtown Boston location. The rapid development of the Route 128 area in the 1970s and

DENNIS O'CONNOR, PAUL BROUDE, AND NEIL ARONSON (LEFT TO RIGHT) HEAD A PRACTICE WITH A UNIQUE FOCUS—VALUE-ADDED LEGAL SERVICES FOR EMERGING BUSINESSES.

THOMAS ROSENBLOOM (CENTER) LEADS A PLANNING SESSION WITH A GROUP OF ATTORNEYS AND STAFF WORKING ON AN INITIAL PUBLIC OFFERING.

1980s brought in a number of the kinds of businesses that the firm represents, including biotechnology, medical technologies, and electronics. While most of its clients are Massachusetts-based and many are considered to be high-technology companies, the firm's dealings extend across the nation and overseas, and its clients come from all over the country and from many industries.

Broude noted that as more businesses search for investors, the firm expects to handle more work with foreign clients expanding or acquiring businesses in the U.S., and with U.S. clients in search of funding and markets abroad.

In characterizing the firm, Broude likened it to the business section of a larger law office. All of the firm's attorneys specialize in the kinds of legal areas that emerging companies frequently need as they plan and grow. These areas include business planning and corporate law, tax and securities, acquisitions and mergers,

financing, and estate planning.

Broude pointed out that from start-up through growth and diversification, the services offered by O'Connor, Broude & Aronson benefit clients in each stage of their development.

The value-added services of business planning and financial advice, which give clients the benefit of the firm's attorneys' business experience and knowledge of financing opportunities, represent an approach to law that O'Connor, Broude & Aronson regards as unique. This approach benefits clients in many types of transactions, whether they are looking for financing, trying to acquire a competitor, or seeking advice about tax planning. The firm prides itself on its ability to help clients structure their dealings advantageously, to introduce clients to potential sources of capital and to explore options for growth.

The high degree of specialization that the firm has achieved and plans to maintain is helpful to the large majority of

O'Connor, Broude & Aronson's clients who, although highly proficient in their own businesses, are not well-versed in the law. The firm recognizes the importance of wedding its technical legal expertise with the business ideas and business goals of its clients; this dynamic relationship is what lies at the center of the firm's work.

The firm's approach also emphasizes keeping clients in close touch with business trends and related developments that might affect their interests. An in-house newsletter, "Emerging Business Update," highlights changes in law, policy, and financing, among other areas. The newsletter offers information about and insights into the issues faced by emerging businesses, in keeping with the firm's emphasis on both traditional legal services and value-added services.

LAWRENCE GENNARI (LEFT) AND ANN BONIS (RIGHT) VISIT A CLIENT'S FACILITY TO STAY CURRENT WITH THE CLIENT'S BUSINESS NEEDS.

In the continuously changing landscape of emerging businesses and entrepreneurs, O'Connor, Broude & Aronson offers its clients the advantage of legal services that combine well-established legal specialties with newer approaches to better serve clients' particular interests, which so often cross the boundaries of standard legal fields or practice areas. This combination has provided the recipe for success for both the firm and its clients, and promises to continue to do so as business and finance continue to evolve.

ANDREW MYERS (LEFT) AND MARGUERITE COCCOLUTO WORK WITH THE CEO OF A SOFTWARE COMPANY ON ITS BUSINESS PLAN.

WESTON, PATRICK, WILLARD AND REDDING, P.A.

WESTON, PATRICK, WILLARD AND REDding, P.A., has an unusual heritage. The firm evolved from law practices that began more than 92 years ago at 84 State Street, in the historic India Building, where it has remained ever since.

THOMAS G. WESTON.

Henry B. Patrick began practicing law at the India Building in 1900, in association with his uncle Elihu G. Loomis, justice of the Central District Court of Middlesex in Concord. The practice focused on representation of private businesses, charities, and estates and trusts.

In a separate endeavor, Thomas G. Weston established his own practice at about the same time and joined with his father in the firm known as Weston and Weston. Shortly after his father retired, Weston moved his practice to 84 State Street, where he began an association with Patrick and Loomis in 1924. Weston, in the meantime, was appointed as a judge in the Newton District Court, a position he held for 25 years. A public-service-minded attorney, Weston also served as an alderman of the City of Newton, a state representative and state senator, president of the Newton National Bank, and trustee of numerous charitable organizations.

HENRY B. PATRICK.

Henry Patrick's son, Loomis Patrick, joined his father's practice in 1930. He spent his entire career practicing at 84 State Street, actively fostering the association's growth. He, too, served as a trustee of many charitable and educational organizations, both in Boston and abroad.

The firm formally organized as a professional association in 1947 and operates as such to this day. It adopted its current name in 1973, in recognition of the contributions made by two of its senior members, Ralph H. Willard, Jr., and George B. Redding. Member attorneys enjoy the flexibility of carrying on distinct individual or group practices within the association, with an array of in-house legal specialists to consult as client needs arise.

Today Weston, Patrick, Willard and Redding is a broadly based general practice firm, representing clients in complex litigation, business, and personal matters, while deliberately remaining limited in size to enable its members to maintain close working relationships with clients.

Members' specialties include civil litigation and appeals, business and charitable organization law, estate planning, estate administration and fiduciary services, taxation, real estate, zoning, insurance, administrative, environmental, aviation, education, employment, civil rights, and immigration law. Such versatility enables the association to provide a wide spectrum of legal services to its members' clients.

FORDHAM & STARRETT

LAURENCE S. FORDHAM AND LOYD M. Starrett established Fordham & Starrett in 1985. The two Harvard-educated attorneys, in partnership with Barry A. Guryan and Brian W. LeClair, organized their business and litigation firm to provide the type of sophisticated representation commonly associated with large firms, but in a small setting that affords clients greater personal attention and efficiency.

With offices at 260 Franklin Street, in the heart of Boston's business district, Fordham & Starrett distinguishes itself as a young firm with deeply rooted expertise. Six partners, two of counsel, and four associates make up the firm, in addition to two paralegals and a support staff.

Fordham & Starrett's practice is general in nature. As a reflection of its size and philosophy, the firm operates without formalized departments dedicated to any one area of law. The firm excels in a variety of fields: civil trials and appeals, corporate and securities law, labor and employment law, commercial law and complex litigation, banking, health care law, lender liability, litigation, international commercial transactions, municipal law, and commercial real estate.

The high quality of the firm's legal services is grounded in the experience of its seasoned attorneys, much of which was acquired at large, old-line firms. Fordham's career encompasses a vast volume of commercial litigation and appellate work, particularly with respect to hazardous and toxic waste, jurisdiction, and securities and tax law. Starrett, a formidable trial attorney, represents interests in the real estate, health-care, and airline industries. His legal expertise spans such areas as securities law, antitrust, labor relations, and employment.

Guryan, a former general counsel of the National Labor Relations Board in Washington, D.C., Office of Appeals and counsel for General Electric Co., has practiced extensively in commercial and products liability litigation and appeals, and has negotiated domestic and international commercial transactions. And LeClair has to his credit a long and diverse list of legal accomplishments in the areas of construction, commercial real estate, landlord-tenant law, and general litigation.

The firm has expanded its partnership ranks by promoting Thomas A. Mullen in 1990, and Robert C. Cadle in 1993. Laurence M. Johnson joined the firm as of counsel in 1991, and Ann E. Johnston was named of counsel in 1993.

In keeping with the emphasis Fordham & Starrett places on personalized legal service, each partner takes an active role in the clients' work, rather than directing energies exclusively to new business development. In a similar vein, all attorneys work on a firm-wide computer network. Computer-assisted legal research and computer-assisted litigation support are integral parts of Fordham & Starrett's approach to working efficiently and effectively on behalf of clients.

SHERIN AND LODGEN

FOUNDED IN 1945 BY ARTHUR L. SHERIN and George E. Lodgen, Sherin and Lodgen originally focused on real estate law and related legal areas. The firm remained relatively small for several decades, moving from 80 Federal Street to 140 Federal Street, and finally to 100

SHERIN AND LODGEN OFFERS ITS CLIENTS SERVICES FROM OFFICES LOCATED AT 100 SUMMER STREET, IN THE HEART OF BOSTON'S FINANCIAL DISTRICT.

Summer Street in Boston's financial district. Beginning in 1982 the firm expanded rapidly, both in numbers and in practice areas, so that in 1993 it numbers approximately 40 lawyers. Much of this expansion was lateral and featured the development of a full litigation group with a wide-ranging practice.

Sherin and Lodgen represents numerous financial institutions, insurance companies, manufacturers, securities brokers/dealers, developers, partnerships, and individuals in a broad range of litigation, including securities defense, insurance coverage, professional and product-liability defense, medical products liability, environmental torts, securities and tax litigation, and debtor-creditor relations.

The firm continues to offer complete representation in real estate and related fields, including a Workout Services Group that offers extensive experience in bankruptcy and insolvency matters. Related concentrations include transactions, financing, corporate organization and acquisitions, and banking and commercial lending. In addition, Sherin and Lodgen provides services in the areas of business law, environmental regulation, construction law, securities representation and arbitration, public and municipal law, taxation, computer law, and personal law.

In its handling of all matters, Sherin and Lodgen stresses meticulous draftsmanship, conservative staffing of cases, communication with clients, and constant accessibility to all clients. The firm also promotes a collegial atmosphere, reinforced by its moderate size, which respects the contributions of all of its members.

In addition to the firm's professional concerns, its members actively participate in local, state, and national bar associations and in other professional organizations.

As it approaches its 50th anniversary, Sherin and Lodgen looks forward to continuing its tradition of thoughtful service in a wide range of areas on behalf of its clients.

STONEMAN, CHANDLER & MILLER

THE FIRM OF STONEMAN, CHANDLER & Miller has represented employers in labor relations and employment law for almost 50 years. The firm provides a wide range of advice and consultation on employment-related issues to clients in both the private and public sectors.

As counsel for management, the firm represents employers before federal and state administrative agencies, including the labor relations boards; discrimination agencies; wage and hour, safety, and contract compliance enforcement agencies; and in alternative dispute resolution before mediators and arbitrators. It assists clients in a wide range of personnel and employment issues, including the review, develop-

ment, and implementation of personnel policies, wage and salary programs, affirmative action programs, development of communication programs and employee handbooks, training programs for managers, and the negotiation and drafting of employment contracts. It also counsels employers facing union organizational campaigns, negotiates and administers collective bargaining agreements, and handles grievances and arbitrations.

The firm regularly litigates cases involving such issues as wrongful termination, discrimination, contract, tort, and other legal claims in state and federal courts.

STONEMAN, CHANDLER & MILLER

99 HIGH STREET
BOSTON, MASSACHUSETTS 02110

(617) 542-6789

TELECOPIER (617) 556-8989

STONEMAN, CHANDLER & MILLER OFFERS CLIENTS EXPERIENCED LEGAL COUNSEL.

TYLER & REYNOLDS PROFESSIONAL CORPORATION

TYLER & REYNOLDS HAS SERVED ITS clients for over 100 years. Today's firm is the successor of the practice of Charles Hitchcock Tyler, founded in 1889 in the old Sears Building at the site of what is now One Boston Place. While for many years the firm was located at One Court St., in 1973 Tyler & Reynolds returned to One Boston Place, where the practice remains.

Charles Tyler brought into the practice a number of distinguished attorneys, including Owen D. Young, later a president of General Electric. Thomas M. Reynolds became a senior partner in 1939, when the firm took its present name. Today the firm numbers seven principals and one associate, as well as two attorneys

of counsel.

The firm's four general areas are corporate and tax; probate, trust and estate planning; municipal and public law; and general litigation. These areas represent the firm's commitment to a full-service practice. The firm has a trust department engaged in administering a number of trusts, an unusual feature in a mid-sized law firm. Historic clients from Boston's business community included The New England Trust Company, General Motors, and Compugraphic Corporation.

Tyler & Reynolds upholds the high standards that Charles H. Tyler made the cornerstone of the practice he began over a century ago.

THE RECEPTION AREA AND CONFERENCE ROOM AT TYLER & REYNOLDS.

DAVIS, MALM & D'AGOSTINE, P.C.

DAVIS, MALM & D'AGOSTINE, P.C., founded in 1979, is one of Boston's newer midsize firms. Starting with five attorneys, it has now grown to 30.

The firm first won recognition in real estate development, land use, and tax-exempt financing. Building on that foundation, its practice has been expanded to include environmental, corporate, international, employment, construction, and securities law, taxation, estate planning, legislation, admiralty, banking and government-assisted lending, and civil litigation.

The comprehensive nature of the firm's practice is best illustrated by its role in recent business transactions, such as land acquisition and tax-exempt financing for the construction of a new South Shore manufacturing facility; engagement by a municipality as special counsel to investigate possible misfeasance by city officals; the enhancement of severance benefits for terminated senior management employees; acting as legislative counsel in the enactment of a Massachusetts statute that protects a client's waste disposal facility; representing a national construction firm in its successful bid for a $200-million public construction contract; representing institutional lenders in eco-

(SEATED, LEFT TO RIGHT) THOMAS S. FITZPATRICK, C. MICHAEL MALM, JULIAN J. D'AGOSTINE, HAROLD R. DAVIS, AND GARY S. MATSKO. SECOND ROW: RICHARD A. NYLEN, JR., FRANK P. CONRAD, KEVIN T. LONG, WILLIAM J. GRISET, JR., MARK E. WALSH, AND CAROL R. COHEN. BACK ROW: ROBERT J. DIETTRICH, CHARLES G. RANCOURT, JOHN D. CHAMBLISS, AND JOHN R. BERMAN. STAIRWAY, FIRST ROW: ROBERT J. GALVIN, JOHN T. LYNCH, AND PAUL E. LEVENSON. SECOND ROW: GROVER S. PARNELL, JR., ROBERT C. GERRARD, AND GEORGE A. HEWETT. THIRD ROW: SIDNEY J. WARTEL, WILLIAM F. GRIFFIN, JR., AND HOWARD P. SPEICHER. FOURTH ROW: LORI H. FREEDMAN, J. GAVIN COCKFIELD, AND LATA BHOPALE WILLIAMS. NOT PICTURED: JUDITH ASHTON, PAUL L. FELDMAN, AND ELLEN DONOVAN McCANN.

nomic development programs sponsored by the U.S. Small Business Administration; counselling a community development organization in the acquisition, financing, and renovation of moderate-income housing; selection (in a competitive process) as special counsel for municipalities participating in loans to small businesses under the HUD Block Grant Program; and, on a nationwide basis, representing clients in the acquisition and disposition of major commercial properties.

In civil litigation matters, the firm's recent accomplishments include a landmark victory in the Massachusetts Supreme Judicial Court clarifying the law of commercial leases; settlement of a major multi-party hazardous waste case brought by the federal government; representation as trial counsel for minority stockholders of a well known supermarket chain involving the largest amount of damages in any commercial case pending in the Massachusetts courts; settlement on behalf of the plaintiffs of a multi-million dollar legal malpractice case; winning a $2-million jury verdict in a disputed merger case; and representing a real estate developers' association in its challenge to fees imposed by a state agency.

In addition to its practice in the United States, Davis, Malm & D'Agostine represents more than 20 Russian and

Eastern European clients. To meet their needs, a member of the Moscow Bar has joined the firm's attorneys, and the Cyrillic alphabet has been added to the word processing system. A unique example of the firm's overseas engagements is its service to the Albanian government in its first national lottery to raise funds for Albania's Olympic athletes.

The firm's progress is a product of the combined skills, experience, and high professional standards of its shareholders and associates with the support of its loyal staff. The firm looks to the future with confidence.

FISH & RICHARDSON

FREDERICK P. FISH, 1855-1930.

FISH & RICHARDSON IS ONE OF THE country's oldest and largest law firms specializing in intellectual property law. The firm originated in New England and, like New England, has undergone major changes since 1878, when Frederick P. Fish first offered his patent litigation services to local corporations. Fish's career spanned five decades and involved him intimately in those technologies that dominated the era: telephone and telegraph, shoes, and textiles. Such was Fish's stature at the height of his career that, having won several major patent infringement suits for American Telephone & Telegraph (whose most famous employee, Alexander Graham Bell, was one of Fish's friends), he was asked by this client to leave his firm to become president of AT&T. After six years at AT&T, Fish returned to the firm, remaining a dominant figure in patent law until his death in 1930.

The firm was small, with fewer than 20 lawyers, throughout most of the twentieth century. Fish & Richardson served traditional, technology-based New England businesses while maintaining its reputation for quality and conservatism.

Then the late 1970s arrived, and in just more than a decade New England's technological focus, and that of the firm, changed beyond recognition. Fish & Richardson rapidly immersed itself in computers and biotechnology, undergoing the most rapid expansion in its history. From 1978 to 1992 the firm grew from 20 lawyers to 55; hired scientists with advanced degrees in computer science and biotechnology; added offices in Washington, D.C., and Houston, Texas; and completely overhauled its infrastructure and practice systems.

During this period, the biotechnology group grew from three lawyers dabbling in the field part-time to one of the largest and most highly trained groups in the country: 13 lawyers and legal assistants, most holding Ph.D.s in molecular biology or biochemistry. Fish & Richardson made history in 1988 by obtaining a patent for Harvard University on a transgenic mouse—the first patent ever granted on an animal. On the other side of the technological spectrum, the firm handles the Fleschmann and Pons patent work on cold fusion for the University of Utah.

The firm's litigators, numbering about 20 lawyers, represent an international group of clients whose businesses range from ski boots to computers to recombinant DNA. Many of the cases handled by the firm's litigators are high stakes by any standard, and in 1991 a team of the firm's lawyers won a patent judgment of $116 million for 3M, the fourth-largest patent damages award in history. Other firm lawyers represented Lotus Development Corporation in one of the country's first software patent infringement suits.

QUINN & MORRIS

THE TREMONT STREET OFFICES OF QUINN & Morris, overlooking Boston Common and the State House's golden dome, symbolize the firm's ties to city and commonwealth. Since founding the firm in 1979 partners Robert H. Quinn and James T. Morris have shaped its character. Quinn served as Massachusetts Attorney General and Speaker of the Massachusetts House of Representatives. Morris was Executive Assistant Attorney General and counsel to the Speaker. Together they ensure that Quinn & Morris clients receive comprehensive representation in governmental relations as well as a complete range of legal services.

Quinn & Morris' diverse clientele includes individuals, small businesses, publicly-regulated industries, and national and international corporations. Firm attorneys have extensive experience in legislative and administrative law as well as government regulation, in which Quinn & Morris is a recognized leader, and effectively guide clients where the public and private sectors converge.

In the complex, sometimes-volatile world of modern business, Quinn & Morris provides strategic representation to clients seeking to meet their goals effectively.

SHAPIRO, GRACE, HABER & URMY

SHAPIRO, GRACE, HABER & URMY concentrates its practice in the area of litigation, with special emphasis on securities law, employment law, environmental law, and general business litigation.

Established in 1981, the firm has eight attorneys, one paralegal, and a support staff of eight people. The firm is well known for its ability to handle large and complex cases in state and federal courts, such as stockholders' class actions, environmental superfund cases, and complicated commercial disputes. Clients of the firm are diverse in their concerns and problems. The clients range from individuals and small businesses to *Fortune 500* companies.

Partners of Shapiro, Grace, Haber & Urmy have taught courses at Harvard and Northeastern University law schools, and they have frequently been asked to teach in continuing legal education seminars. The firm's attorneys have written a number of legal articles, including most recently two chapters in the reference work *Massachusetts Deposition Practice Manual.*

Shapiro, Grace, Haber & Urmy's commitment to the public interest is reflected in its representation of clients for the Massachusetts Civil Liberties Union and the Lawyers Committee for Civil Rights Under Law.

SHAPIRO, GRACE, HABER & URMY PARTNERS, PICTURED LEFT TO RIGHT: TOM URMY, ANDREW RAINER, CAROLYN GRACE, MICHELLE BLAUNER, TOM SHAPIRO, AND ED HABER.

MINTZ, LEVIN, COHN, FERRIS, GLOVSKY AND POPEO, P.C.

MINTZ, LEVIN, COHN, FERRIS, GLOVSKY and Popeo, P.C. is a diverse, progressive law firm of more than 200 attorneys with offices in Boston and Washington, D.C. The firm has earned a superior reputation through 60 years of dedicated, results-oriented performance.

ABOVE: MINTZ LEVIN CHAIRMAN R. ROBERT POPEO STANDS WITH FIRM PRESIDENT KENNETH J. NOVACK.

BELOW: CELESTE SHEFFEY SPEAKS WITH ASSOCIATES KAREN CURESKY AND MARYANN CIVITELLO IN THE RECEPTION AREA OF MINTZ LEVIN'S BOSTON OFFICE.

Today Mintz Levin's practice is regional, national, and international in scope. The firm serves as counsel to high-technology, biotechnology, communications and media, franchising, insurance, real estate development, and energy companies, as well as to major banking and securities firms.

Mintz Levin's practice areas include business law, litigation, international law, real estate law, environmental law, public law, health care, communications and federal relations, labor/employee relations, commercial law, work-outs and reorganizations, government and public affairs, financial planning, employee benefits and executive compensations, and tax law.

"The kind of caring, the kind of thoughtfulness, the kind of history that Haskell Cohn, Ben Levin, and Herman Mintz brought to the firm in [the] early days has continued," Richard Mintz reflected in a welcome address to new associates in September 1992; "Although

we have many, many more people, the value of the personal relationships and the value of recognizing human beings and that we are more than technicians is a special quality of this firm."

At Mintz Levin personal relationships are backed by a high level of legal expertise, by a vast network of resources and technology, by a wealth of professional experience, and by an exacting standard of thoroughness and aggressive innovation that have always characterized the firm.

Benjamin Levin and Haskell Cohn founded the firm in 1933 as a small partnership with a Federal Street office. Herman Mintz joined the firm in 1937, establishing Mintz, Levin and Cohn. During those years the firm's practice concentrated on representing individuals, banks, and private companies; most of the work came through referrals. Ben Levin established a significant reputation for his expertise in labor law, and the firm also developed a special niche in trusts and estates.

Haskell Cohn managed the firm from 1937 until 1964, and it grew as a general practice. Major clients included the Metropolitan Building, theaters and motion picture chains, manufacturing and retail companies, a construction company, the National Shawmut Bank of Boston, Allied Container, and several fuel-oil distributors. Mintz, Levin and Cohn also did a substantial amount of estate planning, probate, and tax planning work.

In 1941 the firm moved to 50 Federal Street and during World War II did considerable work involving government regulation of wages and prices. The immediate postwar years saw new associates, some who joined from law school and some who were returning from military service. From 1955 until 1964 the firm's size remained stable, with seven active partners and five associates. In 1965 Mintz, Levin and Cohn became Mintz, Levin, Cohn and Glovsky, with 10 active partners and six associates.

On January 1, 1968, R. Robert Popeo joined the firm as its first lateral partner. He created Mintz Levin's litigation practice and directed the rapid growth of that practice. In 1971 his name was added to the masthead, creating Mintz, Levin, Cohn, Glovsky and Popeo. (Today the firm's litigator complement of attorneys stands at 55, and Popeo serves as chairman of the firm.)

During the 1970s the number of attorneys doubled, from 18 to 38. In 1979 Mintz Levin opened its Washington office, which by 1981 was headed by Charles D. Ferris, former chairman of the FCC. Ferris' name was added to the masthead the same year.

In 1984 Mintz, Levin, Cohn, Ferris, Glovsky and Popeo moved its Boston headquarters to One Financial Center. Since 1989 the firm has increased its legal staff by more than 25 percent, adding new practice groups to augment its existing capabilities. In 1990 Mintz Levin was joined by 10 experienced health care attorneys and professionals, and added a commercial real estate group of 10 attorneys from the former firm of Fine & Ambrogne. In 1991 the firm's environmental group was augmented by 13 attorneys from Gaston & Snow.

In keeping with its integrated, multidisciplinary approach, Mintz Levin established a consulting subsidiary, ML Strategies, Inc., in 1990 to provide associated professional services to clients needing more comprehensive solutions to their problems. ML Strategies offers services and resources in government relations, public regulatory policy, and community and media relations.

Throughout its six decades in practice, Mintz Levin has remained staunchly committed to community service. Currently the firm's attorneys serve in many responsible capacities in the Boston, Massachusetts, and American bar associations, as well as in numerous nonprofit social service and other agencies. The firm's founders set this precedent from the beginning, serving as trustees at Beth Israel Hospital and the Massachusetts Committee for Children and Youth, sharing responsibility for setting up the Jimmy Fund, and providing legal, professional leadership in the BBA and ABA. Haskell Cohn served as president of the BBA from 1969 to 1971 and as its representative to the ABA House of Delegates from 1969 to 1981.

Mintz Levin is a dynamic, professional practice that continues a tradition of responsive, thorough client representation. The firm is poised to continue this tradition for many decades to come.

LEFT: MINTZ LEVIN'S BOSTON OFFICES ARE LOCATED AT ONE FINANCIAL CENTER.

BELOW: MINTZ LEVIN OFFERS EXTENSIVE SERVICES THROUGH ITS WASHINGTON, D.C., OFFICE.

WIDETT, SLATER & GOLDMAN, P.C.

CHARLES M. GOLDMAN, A FOUNDING PARTNER OF THE FIRM, STILL PRACTICES AT WIDETT, SPECIALIZING IN ESTATE PLANNING.

WIDETT, SLATER & GOLDMAN, P.C., IS A mid-size firm of 47 lawyers, with roots extending back half a century to two smaller Boston firms. Today's firm was formed in 1976 through the merger of its predecessors, Widett & Widett and Slater, Goldman, Gillerman, Shack and Tutun. From its Sixty State Street offices, Widett, Slater & Goldman now provides a full range of legal services to its clients, primarily from business, throughout New England and beyond.

The firm's client base includes *Fortune* 100 companies as well as start-up entrepreneurs, closely-held corporations and small businesses, and individuals with interests throughout the world. Widett, Slater & Goldman clients can count on receiving individualized attention and quality representation through attorney collaboration on the full range of matters that can arise in an increasingly complex business environment.

Practice areas range widely. In keeping with its business orientation, Widett, Slater & Goldman offers departments in banking and finance, business reorganization and creditors' rights, corporate and securities law, domestic relations, employee benefits, entertainment and sports, environmental law, estate and financial planning, government contracts, intellectual property contracts and international contracts, international law, labor and employment relations, litigation, real estate, secured lending, and tax law.

In banking and finance the firm offers guidance in regulatory matters, banking practice, mergers, lending practices, and related areas. Among other areas, the firm concentrates in electronic banking, the establishment of new business ventures, and regular updates of regulatory changes. Widett, Slater & Goldman attorneys represent banking and finance clients before government and industry authorities at both the state and federal levels.

The business reorganization and creditors' rights department offers counsel in formal and out-of-court reorganizations and liquidations for companies of all sizes. Work-outs, dispute resolutions, lease litigation, and all aspects of liquidations and bankruptcy are areas of concentration within this department drawing on Widett, Slater & Goldman attorneys' wide experience in these matters.

The firm's estate and financial planning offers individuals, particularly those with complex personal or business situations, the opportunity to structure long- and short-term arrangements that make use of the firm's attorneys' breadth of knowledge and that take into account the impact on an individual plan of complex factors such as international business holdings, preresidency tax planning, planning for foreign investment in U.S. concerns, or widely dispersed personal assets.

The diversity of contract law has led to recent growth in the firm's offerings in this area, particularly in government, intellectual property, and international contracts. The firm has particularly strong expertise in the federal acquisition area, and it represents a substantial number of government contractors in virtually every aspect of federal procurement law, including negotiations, claims, bid protests, terminations, and government financial matters.

As environmental concerns have become and will remain an integral aspect of business planning and operation, Widett, Slater & Goldman has developed this area to better serve all of its clients' needs. The growing environmental department includes attorneys versed in the layers of regulation surrounding environmental concerns, which gives them the ability to offer negotiation expertise and counsel to clients within this complex and evolving area.

The litigation department regularly calls on attorneys from other areas to assist in delivering the specialized services that Widett, Slater & Goldman clients might need. Among other areas, litigation experience extends to computer and high technology, real estate, antitrust, and financial matters such as SEC investigations and class-action suit defense. The firm also handles a wide range of general business and commercial litigation as well as individual representation in areas such as entertainment and professional sports.

As a relatively young firm, Widett, Slater & Goldman welcomes innovative legal approaches that enhance the quality of legal services offered to its clients. Associates do not have a "waiting period" before they are given substantial responsibility in client matters. Development of practice areas is encouraged, and all attorneys can originate firm clients. There is also less administrative hierarchy than is found in many larger firms, leading to a more collegial model of decision making throughout the practice.

LEFT: HAROLD WIDETT, A FOUNDING AND CURRENT PARTNER OF THE FIRM, SPECIALIZES IN ESTATE PLANNING.

Attorneys from the firm have participated in professional and bar activities at the local, state, and national levels. The firm ascribes to a strong pro bono commitment as well, and both partners and associates engage in a wide range of pro bono and community activities.

Widett, Slater & Goldman, P.C., remains committed to offering all of its clients the full range of experience and creativity that its attorneys bring to the practice, and to keeping up with those legal developments and specializations that promise to impact on its clients and their businesses.

LEON J. GLAZERMAN, THE MANAGING PARTNER AT WIDETT, SLATER & GOLDMAN, SPECIALIZES IN GOVERNMENT CONTRACT AND CORPORATE LAW.

EDWARDS & ANGELL

THE LAW FIRM OF EDWARDS & ANGELL first opened its doors in Providence, Rhode Island, in 1894. Its founders, Stephen Edwards and Walter Angell, were guided by traditional values of superior, efficient legal service as well as a sincere dedication and sensitivity to clients' needs.

Almost a century later, Edwards & Angell continues to hold firmly to these values. From these roots Edwards & Angell has grown into a full-service law firm with more than 175 attorneys.

The Boston office of Edwards & Angell, opened in 1983 with four lawyers, grew to more than 35 attorneys a decade later, and is an important part of the firm's dominant eastern presence. Its unique network encompasses offices in Providence and Newport, Rhode Island; Boston; Hartford, Connecticut; New York City, New York; Newark, New Jersey; and Palm Beach, Florida. Internationally, Edwards & Angell was the first United States law firm to establish formal associations with two Chinese law firms, thereby providing timely service with Chinese legal counsel for clients wishing to do business in the People's Republic of China. Edwards &

Angell's commitment to providing effective legal services is manifested in part through a team approach that maximizes the use of attorneys and paralegal staff within an office and among its offices. In addition, the firm's state-of-the-art communications and word-processing equipment and comprehensive research resources enable it to service clients promptly and accurately.

Edwards & Angell serves clients located nationwide and abroad, with a majority based in New England. Clients include banks, bank holding companies and their subsidiaries, investment bankers, publicly-held corporations, public authorities, newspapers, television companies, cable television and radio station companies, government contractors, venture capital companies, real estate and small-business investment companies, insurance companies, public utilities, colleges and schools, hospitals and other health care providers, and numerous manufacturing companies and small businesses.

Edwards & Angell is as proud of its congenial atmosphere as it is of its high-quality work product. The firm is deeply committed to preserving its strong sense of camaraderie and cooperation. In addition, attorneys in all of the firm's offices have strong community ties and are actively involved in a number of civic, charitable, and professional organizations. This tradition of public service has always been a part of Edwards & Angell's culture and allowed the firm's attorneys to fully appreciate the region's unique economic climate and, in the process, better serve the needs of clients.

ATTORNEYS FROM EDWARDS & ANGELL'S BOSTON OFFICE INCLUDE (FROM LEFT) JED HENDRICK, RICH MCCARTHY, BETSY MUNNELL, DIANE BISSONNETTE, JOE MAHER, JIM MCGINLEY, AND AL SOKOL.

THE TEAM APPROACH IN ACTION, AS PARTNER RICK PERRAS CONSULTS WITH ASSOCIATE JILL HAI AND PARALEGAL JENNIFER HOULIHAN.

LYNE, WOODWORTH & EVARTS

THE FIRM THAT WOULD BECOME LYNE, Woodworth & Evarts opened in 1919. Logan, Lyne & Woodworth was founded by Daniel J. Lyne and Stewart C. Woodworth, Harvard classmates who graduated from the law school in 1912. General Edward L. Logan, the distinguished leader of the Yankee Division during World War I, was invited to join their partnership. In 1923, after Logan left the firm, Richard C. Evarts became a partner, and the firm assumed its present name.

The firm has always stressed the highest standards of professionalism and excellence in representing its clients. Its ethic was recognized by Harvard sociologist David Riesman while he was an associate at Lyne, Woodworth & Evarts in 1935. In a *National Law Journal* interview in 1980, although generally critical of lawyers, he recalled that the firm had "very idealistic people whose attitude was, 'If this is a fraudulent claim, we're going to try to beat it.' Most big firms would have settled such cases."

Another longstanding undertaking of the firm has been the building of community among its people. The concern to perpetuate a sense of community and at the same time be able to serve the needs of an ever-growing list of clients have been the principal guidelines governing the firm's gradual growth.

Service to the public and to the commonweal has always been a top priority of Lyne, Woodworth & Evarts, and over the years the partners have filled a variety of civic and charitable positions with distinction. In 1935 Dan Lyne, with other Boston lawyers, established the Voluntary Defenders Committee, Inc., to afford counsel to indigents accused of crime, almost 30 years before the United States Supreme Court acknowledged that such representation was constitutionally required. This initiative for making lawyers available to the poor was further enhanced by the involvement, for more than 50 years of Edward J. Duggan, now of counsel to the firm, in the Voluntary Defender and Massachusetts Defender committees and the Committee for Public Counsel Services.

Lyne, Woodworth & Evarts has a solid client base, mainly comprising institutional real estate lenders and investors, and life, accident, and health insurers. Over the years the firm has always been in the vanguard of the evolution of the law regulating and protecting its clients.

While serving its clients efficiently and economically, the firm strives to be faithful to its traditions of excellence, zealous advocacy, and commitment to doing what is right.

ABOVE: AMONG THE PARTNERS OF THE FIRM ARE (STANDING, LEFT TO RIGHT) DOMENIC P. AIELLO AND WALTER J. CONNELLY; (SEATED, LEFT TO RIGHT) JOSEPH F. RYAN, JOHN P. CARR, AND JOSEPH H. SKERRY III. NOT PICTURED IS PARTNER WILLIAM B. O'KEEFFE.

BELOW: LYNE, WOODWORTH & EVARTS PARTNERS INCLUDE (STANDING, FROM LEFT) GEORGE E. DONOVAN, EDWARD P. MCPARTLIN, FRANCES X. HOGAN, KENNETH A. JOHNSON, AND RODERICK M. CONNELLY; (SEATED, LEFT TO RIGHT) EDWARD S. ROONEY, JR., NORMAN C. SABBEY, AND NORMAN M. GOLDBERG.

GOODWIN, PROCTER & HOAR

COLONEL ROBERT E. GOODWIN SAW EXTENSIVE SERVICE DURING WORLD WAR I BEFORE RETURNING TO THE FIRM TO RESUME HIS LEADERSHIP ROLE THERE.

ON A SPRING DAY IN 1912, TWO GRADUATES of Harvard College's class of 1901 met on the steps of a Boston bank. Robert E. Goodwin, who had earned his law degree summa cum laude from the Boston University School of Law, was practicing at Carver, Warner & Goodwin. Joseph O. Procter had graduated from Harvard Law School and was an associate at Herrick, Smith. The two chatted, swapping war stories and speaking about their aspirations. As their chance meeting ended, they agreed to further discuss their goals in practicing law. Out of these discussions came a law firm; on July 1, 1912, Goodwin & Procter was opened in the India Building at 84 State Street.

During World War I Goodwin served in the army, seeing almost continuous front-line action as Colonel of the 102nd, and later the 101st, Field Artillery. He received the Distinguished Service Medal with a citation praising his "high standards, exceptional ability, . . . and sound judgment and tact."

After the war, Colonel Goodwin rejoined Goodwin & Procter, which shortly doubled in size with the addition of Fred T. Field and Samuel Hoar. The firm was Goodwin, Procter, Field & Hoar until 1929, when Field resigned to take a seat as Justice of the Supreme Judicial Court. The firm has been Goodwin, Procter & Hoar ever since.

Until shortly before his death in 1971, Colonel Goodwin gave Goodwin, Procter & Hoar moral and intellectual leadership, insisting on the highest standards of integrity and exacting excellence in the practice of law. His example instilled in the firm and its partners an abiding sense of civic responsibility.

After World War II the firm embarked on the growth that characterizes it to this day. In 1969 the firm moved to 28 State Street, where it occupied five floors. On November 25, 1985, it moved into the new, 40-story Exchange Place building at 53 State Street, diagonally across from its original offices in the India Building.

Today Goodwin, Procter & Hoar numbers 270 lawyers, and is one of the largest law firms in Boston, and the biggest U.S. firm with no branch offices. Its total resources and capabilities are located in downtown Boston. Its practice encompasses virtually the entire spectrum of legal problems and specialties, including corporate, commercial, and financial law; a diverse litigation practice in the state and federal courts of New England and elsewhere; a real estate practice that is among the largest and most diverse in Boston; and an environmental law practice that is deeply involved with the most complex and challenging issues in the field in New England and throughout the United States. In addition, the firm actively practices in labor law, taxation, employee bene-

combat the scourge of drug trafficking.

Goodwin, Procter & Hoar has long been an active, responsible member of the Boston community. Individual attorneys are continuously involved in various pro bono activities, and in a wide range

LEONARD WHEELER PRESENTS EVI-
DENCE AT THE NUREMBERG TRIALS
OF ACCUSED NAZI WAR CRIMINALS,
CONDUCTED AFTER WORLD WAR II.

of legal, civic, and community organizations oriented toward the improvement of Boston's community life. In 1987, to recognize the

fits, estate planning and administration, and health care law.

Over the years the firm has had its share of high-profile experiences. After World War II, two partners, Leonard Wheeler and Frank Wallis, were active participants in the Nuremberg trials, prosecuting Nazi leaders such as Herman Goering, Rudolph Hess, and Joachim von Ribbentrop. Partners were also intimately involved in the planning and drafting of, and congressional action upon, legislation in 1960 creating real estate investment trusts. In the 1970s Goodwin, Procter & Hoar was in the midst of litigation arising from the notorious Equity Funding scandal. In the early 1980s partners achieved unique expertise and national recognition for their work throughout the country on Native American land claims cases. In the late 1980s a partner headed a special Boston Bar Association task force on drugs and the courts whose landmark report made major recommendations for legislative and administrative action to

firm's 75th anniversary, the partners created a million-dollar permanent endowment fund, Support for Early Educational Development (SEED). The fund's income is devoted to early intervention programs aimed at improving the educational opportunities offered to the youngest students of Boston's public schools. The creation of SEED was a unique effort among law firms in Boston and, indeed, among law firms anywhere in the United States.

The pursuit of excellence in providing legal services, adherence to the highest standards of professional integrity, and a commitment to the Boston community are the foundations upon which Goodwin, Procter & Hoar was built. These standards continue to guide the attorneys of the firm today, and will be the hallmarks of its future as well.

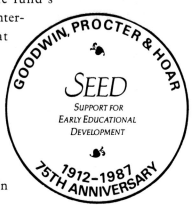

THE PARTNERS CREATED THE MIL-
LION-DOLLAR SUPPORT FOR EARLY
EDUCATIONAL DEVELOPMENT (SEED)
ENDOWMENT TO COMMEMORATE THE
75TH ANNIVERSARY OF GOODWIN,
PROCTER & HOAR IN 1987.

FRITZ & SHEEHAN ASSOCIATES, INC.

SINCE ITS FOUNDING IN 1903 BY HENRY F. Sheehan, Fritz & Sheehan Associates, Inc., has offered the highest level of professional reporting services to its clients.

Originally family-owned, Ethel Sheehan, who married the founder's son, Henry J. Sheehan, still works full time at the firm. A merger with J. Bryan Fritz Reporting Company in 1984 established today's company, which now numbers more than 30 reporters plus support staff.

ED VARALLO (SEATED) DEMON-STRATES A REAL-TIME TRANSLATION ON A NOTEBOOK COMPUTER AS ETHEL SHEEHAN AND BRYAN FRITZ WATCH.

Shorthand reporting dates back to Roman times, when writers used trained secretaries to record their thoughts. Though lost in the Middle Ages, shorthand was revived during the Renaissance and was carried to the American colonies. In the nineteenth century the Pitman and Gregg systems were invented by Isaac Pitman and John Robert Gregg. The perfection of stenography machines made modern speeds possible, while the introduction of electronic technology promises to push court and conference reporting to new levels.

Even the best tools cannot compensate for lack of preparation. At Fritz & Sheehan many reporters receive college degrees before their stenotype training, giving the staff a uniquely high level of general information and vocabulary. Reporters from the company have also fared well in state and national speed competitions, including one four-time National Speed Contest winner and Fritz himself, a two-time Massachusetts speed champion. A third of Fritz & Sheehan reporters have passed all four parts of the national test at the highest speed, and others are on their way; only five percent of all court reporters are so qualified. No other New England court reporting firm can match this record.

Joined to staff excellence is a commitment to introducing and using the latest technologies. Computerized services include litigation support and the relatively new Min-U-Script reduced-size transcripts, available with Word Index, which reduces transcript bulk up to 93 percent, making them more useful than ever to the practitioner. Most Fritz & Sheehan reporters have adopted or are switching to laptop computers, allowing them to provide real-time reporting and the possibility of large-screen and other links through the computer on-site. This potential is especially important for deaf and hard-of-hearing individuals, for whom some of the company's reporters do extensive work. Finally, Fritz & Sheehan also maintains a central file with correct-spelling information from all previous jobs, enabling reporters to arrive better prepared.

Court reporting has come a long way from the wax tablets and styluses used by the Romans. As Fritz & Sheehan marks its 90th anniversary, the firm will be looking ahead to the challenges and opportunities of the dynamic future of court and conference reporting, which promises to benefit all clients using stenographic and related services.

HENRY F. SHEEHAN'S 1903 LEDGER BOOK, ILLUSTRATING THE PRACTICES (AND PRICES) OF TURN-OF-THE-CENTURY COURT REPORTING.

PALMER & DODGE

THE FIRM THAT IS TODAY PALMER & Dodge was founded in 1887 by Moorfield Storey, who was its leader until his death in 1929. A nationally known trial lawyer, he was also a leader of the organized bar, serving as president of the American, Massachusetts, and Boston bar associations. After his college years, Storey had been secretary to the great Massachusetts abolitionist, Senator Charles Sumner. Steeped in that tradition, he was all his life a champion of the disadvantaged, particularly African-Americans. He served as president of the N.A.A.C.P. for nearly 20 years, and he argued and won several significant cases before the U.S. Supreme Court extending minority rights.

Robert G. Dodge, Storey's successor as professional leader, came to the firm in 1910. Throughout a long and notably successful career, Dodge consolidated the firm's reputation as a leader in advocacy at all levels. Continuing the Storey tradition, Dodge served as president of the Boston Bar Association and as a public advocate against injustice in the form of political and judicial corruption.

The third great professional leader of Palmer & Dodge, and the architect of the firm as it exists today, was Alfred Gardner. Gardner believed above all in the delivery of legal services: to clients through prompt and practical attention to their needs, and to the greater community through the organized bar. He was for many years an activist president of the Boston Legal Aid Society, and thereafter of the Boston Bar Association. He served successive governors on issues of prison reform, and he concluded his career as the unpaid chairman of the Massachusetts Crime Commission, appointed by the governor in 1962 to combat state political corruption. In 1967 Gardner received from the Boston Bar Association its rarely bestowed Public Service Award, with a citation observing that, "In the face of criticism, misunderstanding, danger, and strain... and faced with the unrelenting opposition of the strong political and financial power of enemies, yours and ours, you made a brilliant record as chairman."

Gardner's example of service, and his unfailing selflessness and professionalism, set a tone that carried Palmer & Dodge successfully through a period of growth in the 1970s and 1980s. Many lawyers from other firms joined Palmer & Dodge during this period, attracted by its culture of excellence, collegiality, and service. Their contributions, together with the contributions of those whose entire careers have been spent at the firm, have created a large modern law firm with a practice that includes sophisticated corporate transactions; complex civil litigation; representation of educational institutions and other nonprofit organizations, and of private clients; and all aspects of governmental activity and finance, in which Palmer & Dodge is a recognized national leader.

ALFRED GARDNER. PHOTO COURTESY OF THE BOSTON PUBLIC LIBRARY, PRINT DEPARTMENT

WARNER & STACKPOLE

WARNER & STACKPOLE IS ONE OF BOSTON'S oldest leading law firms, striving to meet client expectations of caring, competence, and efficiency. While its standard of excellence is rooted in the expertise and skill of its lawyers, each person at Warner & Stackpole is committed to strengthening client relationships through demonstrations of personal service, such as reliability, accessibility, and responsiveness. This approach enables Warner & Stackpole to deliver both practical legal counsel and client satisfaction—traditions on which the firm's success is based.

ABOVE: THE PRESENT CHAIRMAN OF WARNER & STACKPOLE, SAMUEL ADAMS, IS A FORMER SUPERIOR COURT JUDGE.

RIGHT: PIERPONT L. STACKPOLE JOINED THE FIRM IN 1900, THE YEAR THE FIRM ASSUMED ITS PRESENT NAME.

Joseph B. Warner and James J. Myers began practicing law at 39 Court Street, in November 1874, according to the *Directory of the City of Boston.* They had met as freshmen at Harvard College, class of 1869, and later both attended Harvard Law School. Their three, fireplaced rooms overlooked the courthouse in Court Square, then an area with a very different atmosphere. The courthouse contained the Supreme Judicial Court, all sessions of the Boston Municipal Court, the sheriff's offices, and, in the basement, a police station with holding cells. This site is now occupied by City Hall Annex.

Economic uncertainty following the Civil War culminated in the Panic of 1873, and the times dictated the type of law Warner and Myers practiced. Early cases involved financial default, breach of contract, personal injury, and property damage. Their work was done with the kind of machinery more modern generations would find difficult to appreciate. Telephones, typewriters, and electric lighting were unknown. All documentary work, pleadings, letters, and copies were handwritten; appointments were arranged by messenger or by mail; shelves holding papers and books constituted a library.

Warner and Myers continued to practice until the mid-1890s, when Myers was elected to the Massachusetts House of Representatives. Following Myers' departure, Henry E. Warner joined his brother and the firm was renamed Warner and Warner, with offices at the new 53 State Street building. Henry Warner remained a prominent partner until 1930.

The nature of law practice shifted according to the times and client needs. The large percentage of personal law cases and the firm's customs practice diminished with the enactment of antitrust laws in 1915 and the federal income tax in 1913.

ural gas pipelines built during World War II were inching up the eastern coastline. Since World War II the firm has been active in virtually every aspect of public utility holding company practice, representing individual electric, gas, pipeline, and water utilities.

In its early days Burns, Blake & Rich carried on an eclectic corporate practice at 10 Post Office Square, together with a separate firm in New York. Edmund Blake, former head of the National Labor Relations Board's regional office, strengthened the firm with labor law expertise. John F. Rich, an energetic and talented Harvard Law School graduate, handled much of the detailed preparation and organization of work for corporate clients and took the lead in management of the firm.

At the outset the firm served as counsel to the *Boston Daily Record* and *Sunday Advertiser,* which placed libel cases in the expert hands of Gerald May, Sr., for 40 years. Henry Leen, personal legal advisor to Richard Cardinal Cushing, was also a partner and leading Boston trial lawyer. He later served as a Superior Court judge and is now retired.

The firm lost two of its guiding lights in 1957; Rich became president and chief executive officer of Commonwealth Energy System, and Burns died, leaving a legacy of professional accomplishment and respect among the firm's lawyers. Regrouped as Rich, May & Bilodeau, the firm flourished without changing its level of practice.

Thomas H. Bilodeau, a former Boston Latin School and Harvard football backfield star and an All-American college baseball player, passed up a chance to join the Red Sox in order to practice law. Bilodeau became a vital contributor to the reorganized firm, as he expanded its cor-

porate and utility business and watched over its management. He died in 1987.

Harold Dondis, with the firm since graduating from Harvard Law in 1945, has been active for 40 years in general and utility practice, lately heading a corporate practice team specializing in gas transmission, environmental, and eminent domain areas. Dondis has been the Sunday chess columnist for the *Boston Sunday Globe* since 1964.

Walter Landergan joined the firm upon graduating from Harvard Law in 1953. A corporate practitioner and securities specialist, he is active in the apparel, health care, and transportation industries. He has served as counsel for and director and officer of a number of major, national apparel manufacturers.

GERALD MAY, SR.

In 1958 Harvard Law School graduate Edwin Carr joined the firm. Carr has both corporate and litigation experience and has been in charge of the firm's trial department since 1973. He is active in the retail gas field as general counsel for various companies.

In 1976 the firm changed its name to include that of Arthur Flaherty, a Harvard-trained lawyer who, at that time, was a 17-year veteran of the firm. Flaherty experienced very early success even as a youngster out of Harvard Law School, as an entrepreneur and corporate expert. He now supervises a practice group specializing in securities and corporate acquisitions and reorganization. He has also found time to take a guiding role in the management of the firm and in this capacity carried on the tradition of John Rich and Thomas Bilodeau.

Franklin Hundley, a utility law specialist, joined the firm upon graduation from Harvard Law School in 1963 and heads up the firm's utility law practice group. He is one of the prominent utility lawyers in New England, working in the field of gas and electric distribution and atomic and fossil fuel generating problems. He is on the board of directors of various major utility corporations.

Today the firm is organized according to major client groups, with a view to providing clients immediate and constant access to its highly trained attorneys. The firm's current generation of lawyers takes pride in the standards of excellence set throughout its history, while observing modern approaches to the practice of law.

In the corporate securities area, Joseph F. Sullivan; Daniel T. Clark; Gerald V. May, Jr.; Stephen M. Kane; and Walter A. Wright III are involved in all aspects of business organization, reorganization, securities issuance and regulation, mergers and acquisitions, financing, and trade regulation.

In the utility/regulation area, Michael F. Donlan, Eric J. Krathwohl, James M. Behnke, and James M. Avery have taken a major role in the firm's ongoing representation of major electric generation utilities,

JOHN F. RICH

interstate gas pipelines, and electric, gas, and water distribution companies.

Palmer B. Worthen supervises a group of professionals in charge of the extensive estate planning and probate activities of the firm.

Nicholas A. Kensington works in the area of intellectual property. Kensington and Owen P. Maher specialize in the representation of numerous lenders and real estate owners and developers engaged in the acquisition, development, and financing of major commercial real estate projects.

Michael J. McHugh and Mark C. O'Conner are cornerstones of the firm's litigation department concentrating in the areas of major corporate, commercial, utility, media, securities, tax, banking, and environmental litigation.

GADSBY & HANNAH

SINCE 1963 GADSBY & HANNAH HAS served clients from its Boston and Washington, D.C., offices. Founding partners Paul F. Hannah, then general counsel for the Raytheon Corporation, and Edward N. Gadsby, former chairman of the Securities and Exchange Commission, set out to build a practice for clients from business, finance, and government. Together with four other partners the firm opened offices at 19 Congress Street, with attorney Hannah working not from a desk, but from an old drafting table donated by a business client.

Today Gadsby & Hannah has 50 attorneys in its Boston office at 125 Summer Street and its Washington office at 1747 Pennsylvania Avenue. In addition to its original practice areas in government contracts, construction law, litigation, corporate, securities, and tax, Gadsby & Hannah has developed specializations in areas such as environmental and land use, international law, public finance, trademarks, copyright, intellectual property, and real estate.

The firm represents a number of clients with national and international interests, as well as a range of businesses with regional and interstate concerns. Clients include corporations, financial institutions, public entities, and government agencies, as well as private individuals and organizations.

The firm has broad experience in handling complex corporate matters, including securities offerings, tax-exempt financing transactions, mergers and acquisitions, joint ventures, federal and state regulatory issues, and contractual issues. Firm members have extensive experience in representing public authorities, both as general and special counsel, and a long history of successful advocacy in dealing with state and federal government agencies. On a local, national, and international scale, Gadsby & Hannah is widely regarded in particular for its government contract and construction law expertise.

Attorneys from Gadsby & Hannah have been significant participants in local and national bar associations, holding key committee positions. Two partners previously served as chairs of the ABA's Public Contracts Section and another partner is continuing that tradition.

After three decades of fast-paced business and legal changes, Gadsby & Hannah continues to be guided by the philosophy of its founding partners: to provide superior legal representation, complemented by efficient, cost-effective, and responsive client service.

ABOVE: FOUNDING PARTNER PAUL F. HANNAH BROUGHT TO THE FIRM HIS EXPERIENCE IN GOVERNMENT PROCUREMENT AS AN OFFICER IN THE ARMED FORCES AS WELL AS HIS SERVICE AS GENERAL COUNSEL FOR THE RAYTHEON CORPORATION.

LEFT: FOUNDING PARTNER EDWARD N. GADSBY SERVED AS CHAIRMAN OF THE SECURITIES EXCHANGE COMMISSION.

HAMILTON, DAHMEN & RANDALL

HAMILTON, DAHMEN & RANDALL ATTORNEYS STRIVE TO DELIVER QUALITY LEGAL SERVICES IN A CONGENIAL ATMOSPHERE.

HAMILTON, DAHMEN & RANDALL WAS founded in 1969 by James C. Hamilton and David H. Lamson and has expanded gradually to its current size of eight attorneys. During much of the firm's existence the distinguished and highly respected criminal defense attorney William P. Homans, Jr., was a partner.

The firm has always endeavored to uphold its initial mission of emphasis on the general practice of law in a congenial and supportive environment.

While its client base includes an increasing number of small businesses, the firm remains philosophically committed to providing cost-effective, high-quality individual representation in domestic re[lations], employment, estate planning, a[nd] real estate matters. Litigation has alwa[ys] been an important part of the firm's pra[c]tice.

Hamilton, Dahmen & Randall tak[e] pride in the public service activities of [its] attorneys. The firm regularly does p[ro] bono work in the fields of civil rights, ci[vil] liberties, and discrimination law.

More than two decades after i[ts] founding, Hamilton, Dahmen & Rand[all] continues to successfully build its practi[ce] in a distinctively collegial setting, fosteri[ng] the personal fulfillment of its attorne[ys] and staff as well as the highest level of pr[o]fessionalism in the service of client need[s].

JACK DANIEL COURT REPORTING SERVICES

THE STAFF OF JACK DANIEL COURT REPORTING SERVICES.

BETWEEN OPENING ITS DOORS IN 1988 and doing business today, Jack Daniel Reporting Services tripled in size and continues to grow. That's because clients bring their business back, assured that they will receive the kind of personal attention that Jack Daniel believes sets her court reporters apart from those of other services. A Texas native, Jack likes to bring a touch of Southern hospitality to her treatment of clients. She hires court reporters both for their skills and their ability to give priority to personal service.

Jack Daniel Reporting Services travels statewide and nationwide, and reporters are kept up to date in the latest reporting technologies, such as real-time transcription and related reporting technologies, such [as] video depositions.

Jack provides free diskettes of tra[n]scripts along with hard copies—a valuab[le] "extra" for the increasing numbers of co[m]puterized law offices. Clients also know th[ey] can rely on the firm for last-minute repo[rt]ing; there is always someone on call fro[m] the company's centrally-located offices at [One] Court Square. Jack and her reporters al[so] take pride in fast turnaround times and [in] the appearance of their finished transcrip[ts]. Jack Daniel Court Reporting Services' [re]porters work to provide clients with servic[e] that meet high professional and perso[nal] standards. The growth of the firm bears o[ut] its founder's emphasis on these qualities.

DORIS M. JONES & ASSOCIATES, INC.

DORIS M. JONES & ASSOCIATES, INC., HAS provided court and conference reporting and related services to attorneys since 1979. From a three-reporter business when it opened, Doris M. Jones & Associates has grown to include 33 reporters plus one part-time and four full-time employees, all housed in its 59 Temple Place offices, making it one of the largest court reporting firms in Boston. No matter what its size, however, founder Doris M. Jones wants the company to continue its tradition of service to its clients.

Doris M. Jones has been a court reporter since 1975. Before opening the company, she served as an official reporter for the U.S. Federal Court. She remembers that when she began the firm she was one of the few court reporters to offer computer services at a time when the transition to personal computers in law offices had only just begun.

Today Doris M. Jones & Associates prides itself on keeping up with technological changes. All associated reporters can use computer-aided transcription (CAT) to better aid attorneys with litigation support, and the company provides real-time transcription for a variety of clients. Among other cutting-edge technologies, Doris M. Jones & Associates offers optical scanning of exhibits onto floppy disks, including handwritten texts and visual images, which lawyers can then consult on their own computers. The firm arranges video depositions and related services, including software that links video with real-time transcription and generates coded tape, allowing clients to review coordinated videos and tapes on their own

computers and video screens without additional hardware.

The size of the company makes some of its standards and practices unique. New reporters who have just finished stenotype training are hired for a year-long probationary period, given additional in-house training, and are closely supervised. The company runs its own weekly speed class to keep reporters' skills polished. Regular meetings of the staff keep reporters up to date on technologies and firm standards, and they are encouraged to participate in other continuing education courses and training.

DORIS M. JONES (STANDING) WITH OFFICE MANAGER FRAN SEBESTYEN IN THE RECEPTION AREA OF THE COMPANY'S OFFICES.

Frances Sebestyen handles the complex and important job of scheduling reporters, as well as running the company's front desk. Often the first contact clients have with the company, Sebestyen provides close attention to their needs and, in keeping with company philosophy, always tries to accommodate requests. Thus, while keeping pace with technology and growing to meet the need for services, Doris M. Jones & Associates also maintains its commitment to client satisfaction, a commitment central to the company's growth and to customer satisfaction.

TONI FRANCIOSO (SEATED) GIVES A REAL-TIME DEMONSTRATION FOR FRAN SEBESTYEN, KELLY CHANTIGNY, AND DORIS JONES IN THE COMPANY'S COMPUTER CENTER.

NEW ENGLAND SCHOOL OF LAW

PRESIDENT GEORGE BUSH DISPLAYS HIS GIFT FROM THE STUDENT BAR ASSOCIATION, PRESENTED WHEN HE RECEIVED AN HONORARY DEGREE FROM THE SCHOOL IN 1983.

TRUSTEE CHAIRMAN JAMES R. LAWTON AND PRESIDENT ANNA E. HIRSCH (LEFT) PRESENT AN OIL PORTRAIT TO U.S. SUPREME COURT JUSTICE SANDRA DAY O'CONNOR DURING HER VISIT TO THE SCHOOL IN 1991.

NEW ENGLAND SCHOOL OF LAW WAS founded as Portia Law School in 1908 by attorney Arthur Winfield McLean as the only law school in the world dedicated to the legal education of women. Coeducational since 1938, the law school remains the only Boston school devoted solely to legal education.

For 60 years Portia provided legal education for women at a time when many law schools were closed to them. Dean McLean's mission gained worldwide recognition and its early success is now manifest in the great numbers of women entering the profession every year.

In 1969, under the leadership of Honorable James R. Lawton and a new board of trustees, the school received provisional American Bar Association accreditation, followed in 1973 by full accreditation, which marked the beginning of a period of unprecedented growth. Names that are synonymous with the success of those years are President A. Leavitt Taylor, his successor, President Anna E. Hirsch (class of 1928), attorney Bradbury Gilbert, Dr. Harold Udell, the late Reverend John Edward Thomas, and Dr. Arthur V. Gretchell.

In 1980 the school moved to its present quarters at 154 Stuart Street, which features a state-of-the-art law library and computer center, as well as classroom and office facilities, a dramatic expression of how far the school

had come since its founding with two students in the 53 Tremont Street law offices of Dean Arthur McLean.

In 1983 the school announced the election of Hon. Anna E. Hirsch as president of the corporation. In her honor the school established the Anna E. Hirsch Lecture Series in 1991, welcoming as its first speaker Hon. Sandra Day O'Connor, associate justice of the U.S. Supreme Court. The school also welcomed Vice President George Bush as the principle speaker at the 75th anniversary celebration.

Furthering its historic mission of educating those often unable to attend law school, the school offers day and evening classes as well as a part-time program for students whose primary responsibility is child care. To provide a full range of legal training and experience, the school offers in-house and placement legal clinics as well as clinical options within a number of courses.

The success of its alumni is one indication of the overall success of the school. Historic alumni firsts include the first woman assistant U.S. attorney in New England and the first black woman from Rhode Island to earn a law degree. Currently, alumni members have achieved distinction in a number of areas, including one who serves as Justice of the U.S. Military Court of Appeals and another who has directed the U.S. Secret Service for several years under Presidents Reagan and Bush.

With its unique place in the history of legal education, New England School of Law will continue to serve motivated students of all backgrounds as they strive to join the bar.

AMERICAN ARBITRATION

THE AMERICAN ARBITRATION ASSO-ciation (AAA) is the oldest alternative dispute resolution company in the United States. In an era of overcrowded court dockets and escalating litigation costs, the association believes that there may never have been a better time for parties in dispute to seek arbitration, mediation, of early neutral evaluation in order to resolve their differences.

Two arbitration groups were founded in the 1920s, merging in 1926 to form the present association. The association's 36 offices around the country take a wide variety of cases and participate in thousands of educational and informational programs.

The association offers impartial and trained arbitrators to add their expertise to the proceedings. Negotiations often resolve the issues at hand; if not, parties can move through mediation or binding arbitration. Unlike the legal system, the arbitration process offers greater flexibility, thereby saving time, money, and often anxiety on the part of those participating.

The association has a close relationship with the bar. Locally the Massachusetts Bar Association has given a grant for the Massachusetts Commission Against Discrimination Pro Bono Project to mediate 100 of the state agency's oldest cases with the American Arbitration Association administering the cases. Courts also sometimes suggest arbitration to clients in search of conflict resolution.

The association does not just hear disputes. Its member offices are also called in to design programs for companies so that arbitration or mediation will be in place before problems which lead to disputes develop. Having a procedure forestalls expensive court proceedings and other processes down the line, according to AAA vice president Richard M. Reilly.

The results of alternative dispute resolution can be impressive. Some two-thirds of the cases brought to the association settle before a lot of time and expense are involved. Cases brought under Massachusetts' so-called Lemon Law average 45 days to settle, as opposed to the three years an average business dispute takes to resolve a similar size case in court.

AAA PRESIDENT ROBERT COULSON, PROFESSOR ARCHIBALD COX, ARBITRATOR MARCIA GREENBAUM, AAA VICE PRESIDENT RICHARD M. REILLY, AND JOHN CHURH (LEFT TO RIGHT).

Ending conflicts with arbitration provides another avenue of resolving conflicts in an increasingly complex society. The American Arbitration Association offers this service to interested parties within and outside the bar. Such services can be a valuable parallel track to the more traditional litigation approaches favored by the legal system, particularly as the need for solving problems grows more acute and the availability of courts continues to be limited.

DORIS O. WONG ASSOCIATES, INC.

PRODUCTIVITY HAS MORE THAN DOUBLED SINCE DORIS O. WONG ASSOCIATES, INC., HAS COMPLETELY COMPUTERIZED ITS OFFICE.

DORIS O. WONG, PRESIDENT, ENJOYS A FAR-REACHING REPUTATION FOR EXCELLENCE IN COURT REPORTING SERVICES.

DORIS O. WONG WENT INTO BUSINESS FOR herself as a free-lance court reporter over 25 years ago. Today the company she founded, Doris O. Wong Associates, Inc., enjoys a far-reaching reputation for excellence in court reporting services.

Wong's large, well-trained court reporting staff and attendant support personnel work on all kinds of law suits—from simple automobile accident cases to highly technical and complex business litigation. The firm's ability to produce accurate, high-quality litigation transcripts attracts clients from all over the country. Wong estimates that out-of-state depositions account for about 30 percent of her total business.

Attorneys and law firms that enlist Doris O. Wong Associates most frequently do so for pretrial discovery work, although the firm records such events as court hearings and stockholder meetings as well. In expanding downtown offices located at 50 Franklin Street, Wong and her court reporting staff prepare transcripts by means of computer-aided transcription—all under a rigid, centralized quality control system.

The capability of the firm's court reporters and support staff has served as the backbone of its success throughout many years of growth. Wong, who is accredited to record up to 280 words per minute in shorthand, trains her reporters to meet and surpass tough standards of performance set by industry trade groups. And in the past 10 years, since the advent of the personal computer, Wong has supplemented this talent with technology to heighten the caliber of her firm's services.

Productivity has more than doubled since Wong completely computerized her office. She is always on the lookout for the latest technological advances to serve the legal community. As a result, the firm furnishes such enhanced services as compressed transcripts, which reduce hundreds of printed pages to a manageable handful, and it archives all transcripts on an optical disk, which catalogs all the firm's work dating back to 1990 for speedy retrieval.

"I really like to feel that I'm in the forefront of court reporting. I'm always on the lookout for innovations that benefit my clients," Wong says.

Wong is active in professional organizations. She has served as president of both the Massachusetts Shorthand Reporters Association and the National Court Reporters Association, which awarded her the Distinguished Service Award, its highest honor. She was also a founding fellow, in 1975, of the Academy of Professional Court Reporters. Former governor Michael S. Dukakis recognized Wong's active involvement in the community and legal profession when he declared December 8, 1978, Doris O. Wong Day.

FIRST AMERICAN TITLE INSURANCE CO.

FIRST AMERICAN TITLE COMPANY, Northern New England States, offers comprehensive title insurance services to clients large and small. Founded in 1889, First American began as an abstract company serving newly-formed Orange County, California. Expansion outside the county began in 1957, with a plan for nationwide acquisition of existing companies, negotiation of agency contracts, and establishment of new offices to service every major real estate market. Today First American operates a network of more than 300 offices and 4,000 agents in the United States and abroad, as part of First American Financial Corp., a general holding company.

In New England, First American has operated in Massachusetts since 1971, originally through the Massachusetts Title Insurance Co., the oldest title insurance company operating under its original charter in the nation. Opening as First American in 1978, the company served Massachusetts, Maine, New Hampshire, and Vermont with a three-person staff. Successful in this market, the New England office became number one in gross premiums in Massachusetts in 1986, and number one in all four states served in 1991, a position it has maintained since then.

First American's regional management structure allows title decisions to be made by local company officers, while the national scope of the company gives clients access to single-source title services, among other benefits. Coupled with the flexibility offered by First American's regional plan is the attention to service and client satisfaction that the company commits to its accounts, both large and small. Whether insuring the title of Fenway Park or a condominium garage, whether the property value is $4,000 or $400 million, the company puts client satisfaction first. According to regional vice president Peter C. Norden, the care taken to recruit and maintain a quality staff, including in-house attorneys and salespeople, is the main reason First American can offer such a high level of client service.

First American's experienced staff and longstanding connections to the business of title insurance enables it to provide attorneys with important support in their work. The company plans to continue its growth and expansion through its second century with the same attention to excellence in service that was a hallmark of its

first 100 years, making First American's tradition one that corporate and individual clients can bank on.

FENWAY PARK IS ONE OF MANY PROPERTIES FOR WHICH FIRST AMERICAN HAS INSURED THE TITLE.

Copley Court Reporting

Copley Court Reporting founders and principals Lisa Starr and Karen Cole often describe court reporters as the "silent force" in the law: vital to legal proceedings, but largely unrecognized for their contributions to the legal process.

According to Cole and Starr, the expertise of well-trained, highly skilled reporters is essential in producing the accurate transcripts that both clients and the judicial system demand. Delivering this level of professionalism, they say, led them to leave their former court reporting firm and launch their own business in 1985.

Lisa Starr (left) and Karen Cole are the owners of Copley Court Reporting.

Located at 101 Tremont Street, from the start, in the heart of Boston's financial and legal districts, Copley Court Reporting today reflects Starr and Cole's original commitment to quality. Still a midsize agency despite its growing prestige and success, Copley maintains a talented cache of reporters who, in most cases, have been with the firm for several years.

A pioneer in large-scale home-office contracting, Copley allows reporters to work at home and uses its central office for scheduling and other administrative tasks. This approach enables the firm to minimize overhead and offer clients highly competitive pricing. It has also endeared the firm to talented court reporters, allowing Starr and Cole to provide one of Boston's most loyal and capable court reporting teams.

As administrators, Starr and Cole have adopted complementary roles: Starr handles the firm's most challenging assignments, while Cole manages Copley's daily business activities. Both maintain close relationships with the agency's contract reporters, which each credits as a major reason for the close, cooperative relationships their reporters enjoy today.

Copley utilizes the industry's most advanced technology to provide a full range of services. The firm's reporters are fully skilled in these technologies and routinely attend training sessions to master new systems as they emerge.

In a business reliant on reputation, Copley Court Reporting is among Boston's most highly regarded agencies, and the firm has been contracted by some of the profession's largest and most renowned clients. Starr herself handled the complex proceedings regarding the Queen Elizabeth II's grounding off Cape Cod in 1992. Copley also transcribed scores of sessions for the International AIDS Conference held in Boston.

Lisa Starr and Karen Cole believe that attentive service and a positive work environment will always be the hallmarks of Copley. Inspired by the conviction that technology can never fully replace well-trained professionals, Copley Court Reporting's partners plan to continue their unique role as the silent force behind all of their clients.

CATUOGNO COURT REPORTING

SINCE 1966 CATUOGNO COURT REPORTING has prided itself on meeting the diverse needs of clients throughout the city of Boston, the state, and even nationally and internationally. The company has grown to four offices in Massachusetts and Connecticut with a staff of more than 70.

Founder Raymond Catuogno, Sr., was joined by his wife, Martha, company financial manager; his daughter, Nancy, company vice president and court reporter, who helped introduce computer-aided transcription technology to the company in the 1970s; his son, Raymond Jr., company vice president and court reporter, who helps direct the geographical expansion and technical areas; and his son, George, company vice president and general manager, who organized the company's entry into video depositions and directs the Legal/Medical Transcription Department.

Catuogno Court Reporting handles not only court reporting services, which now include real time (or instant) transcription, mini-transcripts, "key word" indexing, and ASCII and Discovery ZX formats on diskette, but also legal/medical transcription and Sten-Tel transcription. The firm also offers a complete line of video services that include electronic editing and playback in court as well as an integration of video, audio, and transcript. These technologies represent some of the most advanced court and conferencing technologies now available.

Sten-Tel transcription, which Catuogno Court Reporting invented and introduced in 1992, is a transcription service for making verbatim recordings of investigations, meeting minutes, and other open forums in a wide variety of fields. The recording device captures all voices in a room and sends the recording through the handset of a telephone, over the telephone lines and into the firm's audio computers. The staff can prepare a transcript of the proceedings with a same- or next-day return, if needed. Catuogno Court Reporting offers monthly rental of Sten-Tel equipment as well as free training in its use.

The firm offers a complete Legal/Medical Transcription Department to handle the needs of clients who wish to dictate medical reports, legal documents, letters, or notes using the firm's 1-800 phone-in dictation service. This service is available 24 hours a day—from office, home, and even cellular phones. It even offers "same-shift" turnaround for Emergency Room physicians who need to review medical reports while still on shift or for anyone who needs to review a report momentarily after dictating.

Combining cutting-edge, creatively-applied technology with a commitment to maintaining a client-oriented, highly trained staff, Catuogno Court Reporting is poised to remain a leader in the ongoing evolution of court reporting and related services.

THE CATUOGNO FAMILY: RAYMOND F. SR., MARTHA, GEORGE, RAYMOND F. JR., AND NANCY CATUOGNO REINHARDT (LEFT TO RIGHT).

RAYMOND F. CATUOGNO AND HIS SON, GEORGE, SCAN FOR RECORDS ON THEIR DICTATION COMPUTER.

LAWYERS WEEKLY

ASK ANY MASSACHUSETTS ATTORNEY TO name the most important legal institutions of the commonwealth. Along with the Supreme Judicial Court, the state's bar associations, and the Social Law Library, chances are he or she will name *Lawyers Weekly*. Its articles, case summaries, and news briefs are read by more than 90 percent of Massachusetts lawyers, as well as by judges, clerks, law students, paralegals, and others in the legal community. *Lawyers Weekly* has in 21 years become one of the most indispensable tools for attorneys in any field or specialty of the law.

LAWYERS WEEKLY PUBLICATIONS BEGAN 20 YEARS AGO WITH CURRENT VICE CHAIRMAN AND LONGTIME BOSTON LAWYER SAM SPENCER (LEFT) AND FOUNDER AND CEO ED PAWLICK.

The paper began as a four-page publication put together at the kitchen table of founder J. Edward Pawlick in 1972. Pawlick, an attorney with an extensive journalism background, conceived the idea of providing a forum for the legal community to get accurate information about legal issues and important cases in the state. He also wanted to move beyond the compendia of legal notices that made up the existing publications targeted to attorneys.

The result was *Lawyers Weekly* and the response from the legal community demonstrated that the time had come for such a publication. In addition to case summaries and news, the paper soon included advertising for legal positions. It revolutionized the old practice of mailing out firm announcements of new partners, associates, and new offices by giving firms the option of placing those announcements in its pages instead.

The creation of an editorial board in 1978 stimulated discussion of key legal issues in the commonwealth, a function the board performs to this day.

Finally, the wide spectrum of advertisers offering services and products to attorneys has made the publication a primary source of support to all kinds of practices. The information and news presented has made it possible for smaller firms to access resources previously available only to staff-heavy, larger firms, an important consideration in keeping smaller practices up-to-date and competitive.

In 1981 the company founded the Rhode Island edition of *Lawyers Weekly* and since then has founded sister papers in Michigan, Missouri, North Carolina, and Virginia. Continued growth in Massachusetts led the company to relocate to West Street in downtown Boston during 1992, at the beginning of its third decade.

Customer satisfaction has always been a primary goal of *Lawyers Weekly* .

New subscribers can request a refund right up to the end of their subscription. Among other features, the paper includes frequent inserts and special sections on important topics such as office management to help attorneys manage their total practice and career. To increase its ability to help lawyers improve themselves and their practices, the company also publishes books on legal topics.

Since 1992 it has offered an Automated Opinion Service for all summarized opinions, available in mail, fax, and pick-up options 24 hours a day by phone. Every other week the paper publishes a lawyer-to-lawyer referral section as a forum for practitioners wishing to advertise specific legal concentrations.

Lawyers Weekly will soon be available in a computerized format, on floppy disk and/or CD-ROM disk. Keeping up with computer technology will, publisher Dan Sharp believes, keep *Lawyers Weekly* on the cutting edge for working attorneys.

The company also publishes a national edition. Targeted to the creative attorney ready to make use of trends in the courts and among other practitioners, the national edition works to get information about the cutting edge of law to its readers. It includes summaries of all U.S. Supreme Court opinions as well. Among the legal trends the national edition accurately highlighted were the use of RICO in business fraud cases and the filing of lawsuits against cigarette companies alleging liability in instances of lung cancer among smokers.

LOCAL ATTORNEYS, PARALEGALS, AND CLERKS ARE OFTEN FOUND DOING QUICK RESEARCH IN THE LOBBY OF LAWYERS WEEKLY PUBLICATIONS AT 41 WEST STREET, BOSTON.

Much has changed for *Lawyers Weekly* from the time it began on Ed Pawlick's kitchen table. Despite growth, moves, and change, however, the intertwined goals of *Lawyers Weekly* remain service to attorneys and service to the entire legal structure of the commonwealth. As the practice of law continues to change, *Lawyers Weekly* and its sister publications will, vice chairman Sam Spencer and publisher Sharp agree, keep up the pace. Their goal, and the goal of everyone connected with the enterprise, is to keep *Lawyers Weekly* as relevant to attorneys as it has always been, and to serve the varied needs of the Massachusetts bar.

ATTORNEYS IN SIX STATES NOW LOOK TO *LAWYERS WEEKLY* AS THE SOURCE FOR THE MOST RECENT COURT DECISIONS. A NATIONAL EDITION IS ALSO GAINING PROMINENCE.

NEW ENGLAND LEGAL SEARCH

FOR MORE THAN A DECADE, NEW England Legal Search has provided law firms, corporations, and attorneys with superior quality placement services. Whether assisting firms in finding partners or associates, and whether the scope of placement involves individuals, departments, or entire firms, New England Legal Search serves a varied, dynamic clientele.

Founder Dee McMeekan and her partner, Linda Kline, both attorneys, bring legal experience and an extensive network of professional contacts to their

LINDA J. KLINE, ESQ., (LEFT), AND DEE B. MCMEEKAN, ESQ.

business. McMeekan graduated from Tulane University School of Law and was formerly associated with the Washington, D.C., office of Seyfarth, Shaw, Fairweather & Geraldson. Kline, a cum laude graduate of Georgetown University Law Center, where she served on the editorial board of the *Georgetown Law Review*, was a law clerk on the United States First Circuit Court of Appeals and was then associated with Nutter, McClennen & Fish.

Clients of New England Legal Search rely on the company's outstanding level of personal service. One or both partners routinely meet with clients before candidate screening begins. They assist their clients in formulating a hiring strategy. Once the scope of their search is determined, individuals with appropriate

credentials are interviewed. The company maintains both client position descriptions and candidate resumes on a computerized data base to increase search efficiency. Such attention adds to the overall success rate of New England Legal Search, which was ranked the number-one legal recruiter in New England in the most recent survey conducted by *The American Lawyer*. Both McMeekan and Kline believe in adhering to strict standards of discretion and ethical practice. Clients and candidates can rest assured that their confidentiality will be maintained. The organization adheres to the Code of Ethics of the National Association of Legal Search Consultants, of which New England Legal Search is a founding member and McMeekan is a past vice president.

While New England Legal Search, as its name implies, serves the New England region primarily, the partners maintain an active nationwide network which allows them to refer clients and candidates to other reputable placement agencies across the country. The partners also have international contacts. Naturally they also receive numerous referrals and calls from candidates interested in positions in this region.

New England Legal Search provides a key service to Boston's legal community. Dee McMeekan and Linda Kline's commitment to the highest standard of professionalism ensures both client and candidate satisfaction. They look forward to building on this tradition of service and proven performance as they enter their second decade of attorney placement.

PARTNERS IN EXCELLENCE INDEX

SPONSORS

CONTRIBUTORS

DISCOVERING THE PUBLIC INTEREST
A History of the Boston Bar Association

By Douglas Lamar Jones,
Alan Rogers, James J. Connolly,
Cynthia Farr Brown, and Diane Kadzis

Picture Research by Cynthia Farr Brown

Edited by Jeffrey Book, Nancy Jackson

Senior Editor, Jeffrey Reeves

Designed by Jonathan Wieder

Photo Editor, Robin L. Sterling

Managing Editor: Linda J. Hreno. *Assistant Editor:* Michael P. Macuk. *Coordinator:* Kelly Goulding. *Proofreader:* Martha Cheresh. *Editorial Assistant:* Kimberly J. Pelletier. *Assistant Coordinators:* Keith Martin, Erin Goulding.

Production Manager: Jeffrey Scott Hayes. *Art Production:* Amanda Howard. *Manager, Computer Systems*: Steve Zehngut.

Sales and Marketing: Nellie C. Scott

Copyright © 1993 CCA Publications, Inc. All rights reserved, including the right of reproduction in whole or in part in any form. Printed in the United States of America.

Published in cooperation with the Boston Bar Association by CCA Publications, Inc., 7355 Topanga Canyon Boulevard, Suite 202, Canoga Park, CA 91303 (818) 710-1627.

Library of Congress Cataloging-in-Publication Data

Discovering the public interest : a history of the Boston Bar Association / Douglas
    Lamar Jones ... [et al.].
        p. cm.
    Includes bibliographical references and index.
    ISBN 1-884166-00-8 : $29.95
        1. Boston Bar Association—History. I. Jones, Douglas Lamar, 1944– .
    KF334.B67B6743 1993
    340'.06'074461—dc20

93-20601
CIP